CW00363704

CHARMING
SMALL·HOTEL
GUIDES

Spain

CHARMING SMALL HOTEL GUIDES

Spain

Including: Mallorca, Menorca, Ibiza, Formentera

Edited by Nick Inman

DUNCAN PETERSEN

HUNTER
PUBLISHING

Copyright   © Duncan Petersen Publishing Ltd 1998

Conceived, designed and produced by
Duncan Petersen Publishing Ltd.

Editor Nick Inman
Associate editor Clara Villanueva
Revisions editor Nicola Davies
Art director Mel Petersen
Maps Christopher Foley

This edition published in the UK and Commonwealth 1998 by
Duncan Petersen Publishing Ltd,
31 Ceylon Road, London W14 OPY
Reprinted 1999

Sales representation and distribution in the U.K. and Ireland by
Portfolio Books Limited
Unit 1c, West Ealing Business Centre
Alexandria Road
London W13 ONJ
Tel: 0181 579 7748

A CIP catalogue record for this book is available
from the British Library

ISBN 1 872576 87.7

AND

Published in the USA 1999 by
Hunter Publishing Inc.,
130 Campus Drive, Edison, N.J. 08818
Tel (908) 225 1900 Fax (908) 417 0482

ISBN 1-55650-829-8

Originated by Reprocolor International S.R.I., Milan
Printed by G. Z. Printek, Spain.

Contents

Introduction

This guide to Spanish hotels – completely updated for 1998-9 – is part of a series that now covers more than a dozen destinations – for details see the back cover.

Charming and small

There really are relatively few *genuine* charming small hotels. Unlike other guides, we are particularly fussy about size. In Spain, even family-run hotels seem to grow inevitably, and the ten-room hotel is a rarity, but most of our recommendations have fewer than 30 rooms. If a hotel has more than that, it needs to have the feel of a much smaller place to be in this guide.

We attach more importance to size than other guides because we think that unless a hotel is small, it cannot give a genuinely personal welcome, or make you feel like an individual, rather than just a guest. For what we mean by a personal welcome, see below.

Unlike other guides, we often rule out places that have great qualitites, but are nonetheless no more nor less than – hotels. Our hotels are all special in some way.

We think that we have a much clearer idea than other guides of what is special and what is not; and we think we apply these criteria more consistently than other guides because we are a small and personally managed company rather than a bureaucracy. We have a small team of like-minded inspectors, chosen by the editor and thoroughly rehearsed in recognizing what we want. While we very much appreciate readers' reports - see below - they are not our main source of information.

Last but by no means least, we're independent – there's no payment for inclusion.

So what exactly do we look for?
• An attractive, preferably peaceful setting.
• A building that is either handsome or interesting or historic, or at least with a distinct character.
• Ideally, we look for adequate space, but on a human scale: we don't go for places that rely on grandeur, or that have pretensions that could intimidate.
• Decoration must be harmonious and in good taste, and the furnishings and facilities comfortable and well maintained. We like to see interesting antique furniture that is there because it can be used, not simply revered.
• The proprietors and staff need to be dedicated and thoughtful, offering a personal welcome, without being intrusive. The guest needs to feel like an individual.

Spanish hotels, large and small

Small hotels have always had the special appeal that they can offer the traveller a personal welcome and personal

Introduction

attention, whereas larger places are necessarily more institutional. In Spain, this distinction is particularly valid. The establishments described in this guide are simply the 200 or so hotels, guest-houses, inns and bed-and-breakfast places that we believe most discriminating travellers would prefer to stay in, given the choice. About 160 hotels are described in detail, in full entries of a page or half a page; the remainder are covered in two other ways. First, in each major regional section there is a feature box devoted to the Paradores of that region; Paradores are a uniquely Spanish institution, described in detail later in this introduction. Secondly, for some areas where we are conscious that there are many hotels other than our entries that a traveller might like to know about, we have included an area introduction summarising some of those hotels.

Of course, not every hotel included here has all the attributes we list opposite. And, to be frank, we have been disappointed by the standards of some Spanish hotels compared with those of France, Italy and the British Isles; in Spain, hotels that approach our ideal are few, and far between. The buildings Spanish hotels occupy are often splendid, and all the hotels listed here are at least adequately run; but you rarely encounter the really excellent family-run hotel which has long been such an essential element of the hotel scene in France and Italy, and is now evident in the British Isles. However, several such hotels have opened in Spain since the first edition of this guide was published in 1991 and we are confident that staying in any of the hotels recommended here will enrich any trip through Spain – and our descriptions make clear which ones are the happy exceptions to the rule.

Reporting to the guide
The *Charming Small Hotel Guides* are greatly strengthened by reports from people who have stayed in the hotels recommended in them, or who have found other places which seem to deserve an entry. Particularly helpful reporters earn a free copy of the next edition of the guide concerned. On page 11 is further information about reporting to the guide.

How to find an entry
In this guide, the entries are arranged by province, and the provinces are clustered in convenient regional groups. The regions, and within them the provinces, are arranged in a sequence starting in the extreme north-west (La Coruña) and working west to east and north to south. The Balearic Islands (Mallorca and its neighbours) come last in the sequence.

Introduction

Paradores

The state-run chain of Paradores dominates the Spanish hotel scene just as many of the castles the hotels occupy dominate the surrounding landscape. They are not the best hotels in Spain, and few of them are notably good by absolute standards – though in any given locality the Parador is quite likely to be the best in town, for the simple reason that many have been created in areas which private enterprise might not find attractive. But Paradores do have great attractions: many are set in wonderfully atmospheric old buildings – mansions, convents, hunting lodges as well as magnificent castles – and many others have spectacular mountain settings. Others are simply very convenient for the traveller on the road, being strategically positioned to fill gaps on the map of Spain.

In terms of their qualities as places to stay, Paradores are much less impressive. Their strong point, usually, is the bedrooms, which are normally very spacious and well furnished. Public rooms may be comfortable and inviting, but may equally be dismally furnished and gloomy. Food, which aims to reflect regional traditions, may be highly satisfactory or extremely ordinary. Service is equally unpredictable, and seems to depend more on individual initiative than any management policy.

Parador room prices vary widely (unlike meal prices, which are almost uniform). In the tourist Mecca of Granada, for example, you pay over three times what you pay in remote mountain areas; in most established tourist haunts – Toledo, Córdoba or Santillana del Mar, say – you pay something between these extremes.

Are they worth these prices? For most people, we judge that the answer is a qualified yes. The best of the Paradores – which you will be able to identify from our descriptions and photographs – really can add something to your travels. But we would not recommend planning a trip entirely around Paradores; not only would the cost mount up alarmingly, but the drawbacks of these somewhat inconsistent establishments might begin to weigh more heavily, while the special appeal that they have might begin to pall.

In our entries, we have abbreviated the proper name Parador de Turismo de España to the letters PT.

Introduction

To find a hotel in a particular area, simply browse through headings at the top of the pages until you find that area – or use the maps following this introduction to locate the appropriate pages. To locate a specific hotel or a hotel in a specific place, use the indexes at the back, which lists the entries alphabetically, first by name and then by place-name.

How to read an entry
At the top of each entry is a coloured bar highlighting the name of the town or village where the establishment is located, along with a categorization which gives some clue to its character. These categories are, as far as possible, self-explanatory.

The letters PT in the name of a hotel stand for Parador de Turismo de España (see opposite).

Fact boxes
The fact box given for each hotel follows a standard pattern which requires little explanation; but:

Under **Tel** we give the telephone number starting with the area code used within the country; when dialling from another country, omit the initial 9 of this code.

Under **Location** we give information on the setting of the hotel and on its car parking arrangements, as well as pointers to help you find it.

Under **Food & drink** we list the meals available.

Prices
We use price bands rather than figures:

P	less than 5,000 pesetas
PP	5,000-10,000 pesetas
PPP	10,000-13,000 pesetas
PPPP	over 13,000 pesetas

Normally we give the range of prices you can expect to pay for a room, including tax and service – from the cost of the cheapest single room in low season to the cost of the dearest double in high season. Wherever possible we have given prices for 1998-99, but prices may be higher in 1999 than those quoted because of inflation. But bear in mind also that the proprietors of hotels and guest-houses may change their prices from one year to another by much more than the rate of inflation. Always check when booking.

After the room price, we normally give the prices of

Introduction

breakfast and other meals. If room-only or bed-and-breakfast terms are not available, we give either the price for dinner, bed and breakfast (DB&B), or for full board (FB) – that is, all meals included:

P   less than 1,5000 pesetas
PP   1,500-4,000 pesetas
PPP   over 4,000 pesetas

Under **Rooms** we summarize the number and style of bedrooms available. Our lists of facilities in bedrooms cover only mechanical gadgets.

Under **Facilities** we list public rooms and then outdoor and sporting facilities which are either part of the hotel or immediately on hand; facilities in the vicinity of the hotel but not directly connected with it (for example, a nearby golf course) are not listed here, though they sometimes feature at the end of the main description in the **Nearby** section, which presents a selection of interesting things to see or do in the locality.

We use the following abbreviations for **Credit cards**:
   AE American Express DC Diners Club
   MC MasterCard (Access/Eurocard)
   V Visa (Barclaycard/Bank Americard/Carte Bleue etc)

The final entry in a fact box is normally the name of the proprietor(s); but where the hotel is run by a manager we give his or her name instead.

Reporting to the guides

Please write and tell us about your experiences of small hotels, guest-houses and inns, whether good or bad, whether listed in this edition or not. As well as hotels in Spain, we are interested in hotels in Britain and Ireland, Italy, France, Portugal, Austria, Switzerland, Germany and other European countries, and those in the eastern United States.

The address to write to is:

The Editor,
c/o Duncan Petersen Publishing Ltd,
31 Ceylon Road,
London W14 OPY.

Checklist
Please use a separate sheet of paper for each report; include your name, address and telephone number on each report.

Your reports will be received with particular pleasure if they are typed, and if they are organized under the following headings:

Name of establishment
Town or village it is in, or nearest
Full address, including post code
Telephone number
Time and duration of visit
The building and setting
The public rooms
The bedrooms and bathrooms
Physical comfort (chairs, beds, heat, light, hot water)
Standards of maintenance and housekeeping
Atmosphere, welcome and service
Food
Value for money

We assume that in writing you have no objections to your views being published unpaid, either verbatim or in an edited version. Names of major outside contributors are acknowledged, at the editor's discretion, in the guide.

Hotel location maps

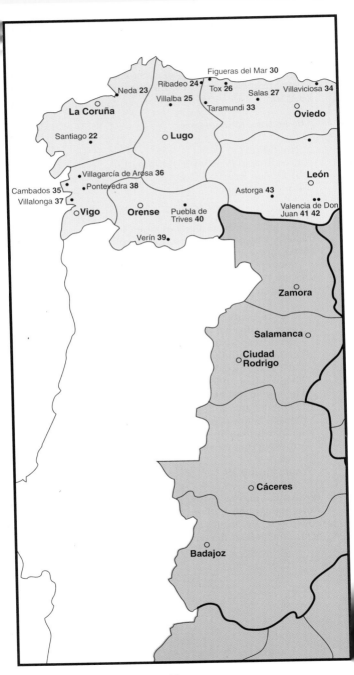

Hotel location maps

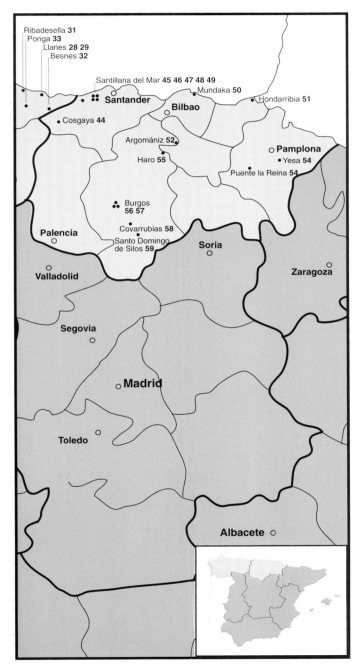

Ribadesella **31**
Ponga **33**
Llanes **28 29**
Besnes **32**

Santillana del Mar **45 46 47 48 49**
Mundaka **50**
Hondarribia **51**

Santander
Bilbao

Cosgaya **44**

Argomániz **52**
Pamplona
Yesa **54**
Haro **55**
Puente la Reina **54**

Burgos
56 57

Covarrubias **58**
Santo Domingo
de Silos **59**
Soria

Palencia

Valladolid
Zaragoza

Segovia

Madrid

Toledo

Albacete

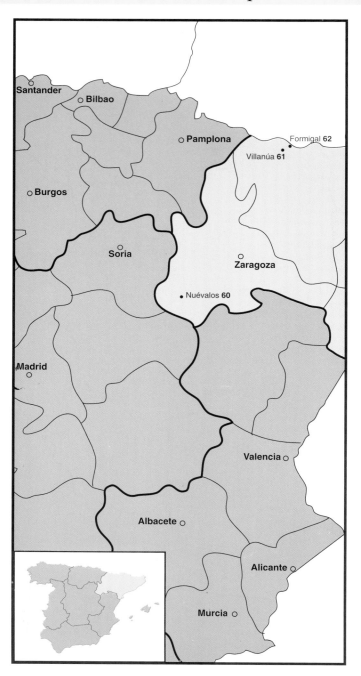

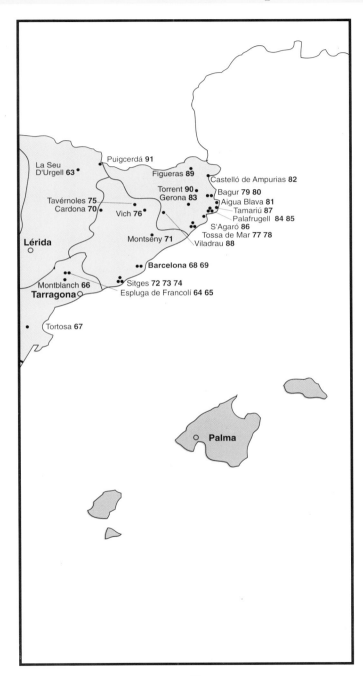

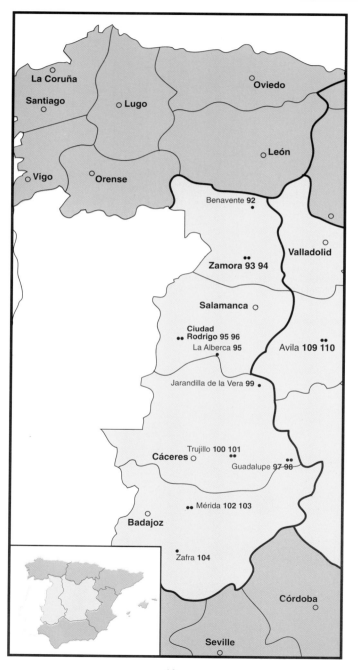

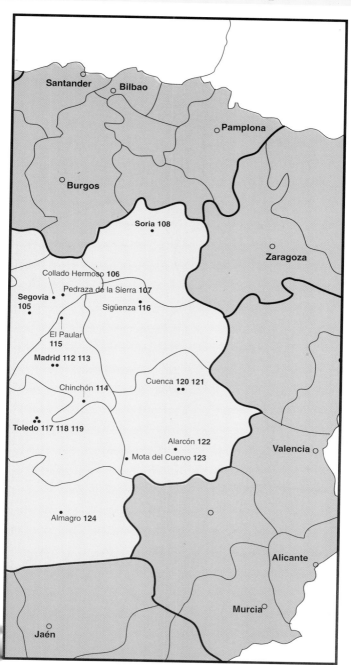

Santander
Bilbao
Pamplona
Burgos
Soria 108
Zaragoza
Collado Hermoso 106
Pedraza de la Sierra 107
Segovia
105
Sigüenza 116
El Paular
115
Madrid 112 113
Chinchón 114
Cuenca 120 121
Toledo 117 118 119
Alarcón 122
Valencia
Mota del Cuervo 123
Almagro 124
Alicante
Murcia
Jaén

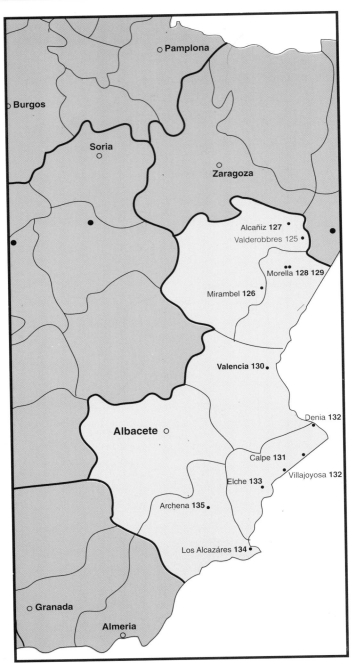

Pamplona

Burgos

Soria

Zaragoza

Alcañiz **127**
Valderobbres **125**

Morella **128 129**

Mirambel **126**

Valencia **130**

Denia **132**

Albacete

Calpe **131**

Villajoyosa **132**

Elche **133**

Archena **135**

Los Alcazáres **134**

Granada

Almeria

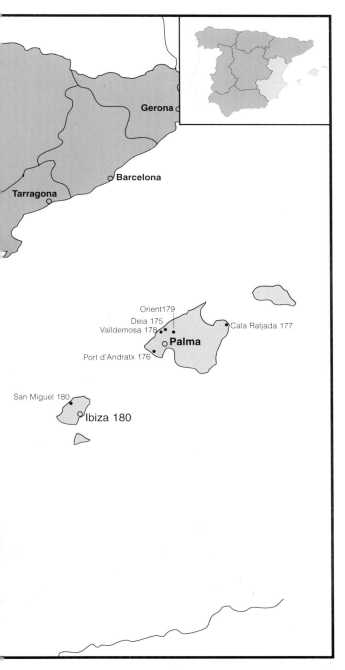

Gerona

Barcelona

Tarragona

Orient179
Deia 175
Valldemosa 178
Palma
Port d'Andratx 176
Cala Ratjada 177

San Miguel 180
Ibiza 180

Hotel location maps

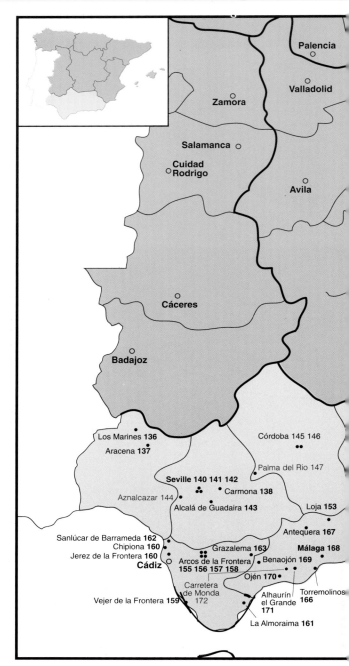

Palencia

Valladolid

Zamora

Salamanca

Cuidad
Rodrigo

Avila

Cáceres

Badajoz

Los Marines **136**
Aracena **137**

Córdoba 145 146

Palma del Rio 147

Seville 140 141 142
• Carmona **138**

Aznalcazar 144
Alcalá de Guadaira **143**

Loja **153**

Antequera **167**

Sanlúcar de Barrameda **162**
Chipiona **160**
Jerez de la Frontera **160**
Cádiz

Grazalema **163**

Málaga 168

Arcos de la Frontera
155 156 157 158

Benaojón **169**

Ojén **170** •

Carretera
de Monda
172

Alhaurín
el Grande
171

Torremolinos
166

Vejer de la Frontera **159**

La Almoraima **161**

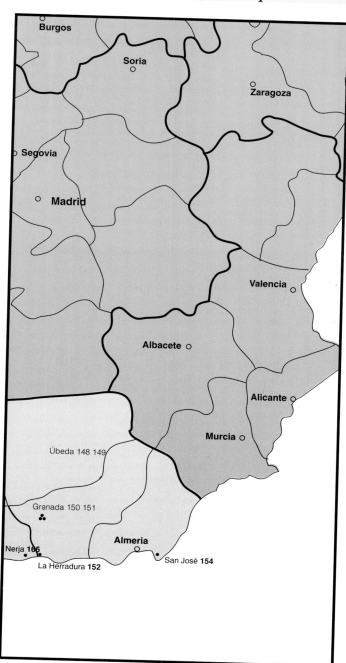

La Coruña

La Estela

Santiago, with its relics of St James, has attracted pilgrims for centuries, and today people come for the beautifully preserved old city with its cathedral, squares and museums. This tiny, family-run *hostal* is tucked away in a corner right opposite one of Spain's most grand and opulent hotels (Los Reyes Católicos, now part of the Parador chain) – a rather interesting contrast, particularly if you compare prices. There is no restaurant here but the surrounding streets are packed with places to eat. The rooms are very basic but they are clean and quite adequate for a night's stop.

Nearby Cathedral, Old Town and the Hospital Real.

Rajoy No 1, 15705, Santiago de Compostela, La Coruña
Tel (981) 582796
Location in heart of old town, by Parador and cathedral; no private car parking
Prices rooms P; breakfast P
Rooms 5 double, 4 with washbasin, 1 with bath; 9 single, 3 with washbasin, 6 with bath; all rooms have central heating

Credit cards not accepted
Children welcome
Disabled no special facilities
Pets accepted
Closed never
Proprietor Eduardo Pedrido

Paradores in North-west Spain

North-west Spain has more than its fair share of Paradores – and some of these are small and charming enough to have earned detailed entries . The province of Pontevedra (bordering Portugal on the west coast) is particularly well endowed, with four Paradores within a hundred kilometres of one another. The largest of these (124 rooms), the PT Conde de Gondomar at Bayona, is a smart modern hotel built within the walls of an ancient fortress. It has all the classic ingredients – crenellated walls, pillared balconies, an open courtyard, richly decorated rooms, beautifully manicured lawns and spectacular views of the Ría de Vigo (Tel (986) 355000). By local standards Bayona is expensive, but it does not even come close to the Reyes Católicos in Santiago de Compostela – one of the most expensive Paradores, but also one of the most superior and most historic, built in the 15th century to house pilgrims from all over Europe who came to pay homage at the shrine of St James in Santiago's magnificent cathedral (Tel (981) 582200). Beware 25th July: this is the feast day of St James, and the city (and Parador) are packed.

Léon's central 253-room Parador, San Marcos, notable for its fabulous façade and two-storey cloisters and once a watering-hole on the pilgrim route to Santiago, is now a smart hotel, laden with antiques and surrounded by formal gardens (Tel (987) 237300).

La Coruña

Pazo da Merced

Neda is a town full of beautiful old mansions, and this hotel, built of dressed stone, and with its own adjacent chapel, dedicated to the Virgen de la Merced (Our Lady of Mercy), is housed in one of them.

The *pazo* or country manor house, was built in the 17thC and sits in open countryside on the low-lying green shore at the head of the Ría del Ferrol.

A few years ago, the owners, facing bankruptcy, decided to sell it to an architect specializing in the restoration of old buildings. With patience and skill, he has turned it into a magnificent rural hotel which combines respect for the historic architecture with a certain originality in the use of materials. His wife, Marinela Medina, has taken charge of the management of the hotel.

The *pazo* only has five rooms, but they are well furnished and equipped with all that you could need. The service is welcoming and diligent: every guest is made to feel at home.

Through the windows you can see Couto monastery, with which the Pazo used to be connected by a tunnel underneath the water. The hotel makes a convenient base from which to visit this and other local examples of Romanesque architecture.
Nearby San Felipe castle (9 km); La Palma castle (14 km).

15510, Neda, La Coruña
Tel (981) 382200
Fax (981) 380104
Location on the Ría del Ferrol, by the waterside; with garden and car parking
Meals breakfast
Prices rooms PP-PPP; breakfast P
Rooms 5 double, all with bath; all rooms have central heating, TV, minibar,
telephone, hairdrier
Facilities swimming-pool
Credit cards AE, DC, MC, V
Children very welcome
Disabled access difficult
Pets not accepted
Closed never
Proprietor Marinela Medina

Lugo

Modern Parador, Ribadeo

PT de Ribadeo

Ribadeo is now reached by an elegant road bridge which spans the mouth of the *ria* effectively bypassing the more picturesque towns of Figueras and Castropol which used to lie en route. The Parador finds itself in a quiet backwater of the town since the change in the traffic flow, but it is only a short walk into the town centre.

The building itself is nothing special and parts of it are showing their age. It overlooks the harbour which has the usual array of fishing boats, from one-man ventures to larger deep sea vessels, all bringing their catches right to the door. There is also a mineral-loading quay which can make clouds of dust if the wind is blowing the wrong way. The restaurant here, as you would expect, has an interesting selection of fish on the menu –also soups, salads, *hors d'oeuvres*, grills and stews.

The atmosphere here is informal, friendly and relaxed while offering all the more home-like Parador standards. One comment from a guest was surprise at the lack of spoken English on the reception desk, particularly as so many British use this hotel on their way to and from Galicia via Santander.

Nearby Early Romanesque Church of San Martín de Mondoñedo, near Foz (23 km); Los Castros beach (5 km).

Amador Fernández s/n, 27700, Ribadeo, Lugo
Tel (982) 128825
Location above harbour in quiet part of town; with garden, garage and car parking
Meals breakfast, lunch, dinner
Prices rooms PP-PPPP; breakfast P; dinner PPP
Rooms 42 double, 5 single, all with bath; all rooms have central heating, phone, TV, minibar
Facilities dining-room, sitting-room, 2 other sitting-areas, bar
Credit cards AE, DC, MC, V
Children welcome
Disabled access easy; 2 ground-floor rooms
Pets not accepted
Closed never
Manager Eligio Dominguez

Lugo

Historic Parador, Villalba

PT Condes de Villalba

This is one of the smallest and most interesting of the Paradores. There are only six rooms, so it is as well to book ahead, particularly in the busiest summer months.

The octagonal tower of Los Andrade stands high above the little town of Villalba, surrounded by the old cobbled streets and squares of the original village, looking out over pleasant rolling countryside. Ask for the key to the roof area for a fabulous all-round view.

The walls of the building are something over six feet thick, and the only window to your room will probably be a tiny arrow slit, so even the all-night celebrations of midsummer, with street parties, fireworks and bonfires, will not keep you awake. In the morning the screeching of swifts and the cheeping of sparrows will be the only sounds to reach you when you open your shutters.

The dining-room is in the cellars, down a grand staircase, with a huge fireplace, wrought iron chandeliers and the atmosphere of a baronial hall, even though it is not huge. The wines and food reflect the produce of the area with, for once, a generous selection of salads and fresh fruit.

Nearby Lugo (36 km), the ancient walled provincial capital.

Valeriano Valdesuso s/n,
27800, Villalba, Lugo
Tel (982) 510011
Fax (982) 510090
Location in heart of old part of town, with garden; parking for 5 cars
Meals breakfast, lunch, dinner
Prices rooms PPP; breakfast P; lunch and dinner PP
Rooms 6 double, all with bath; all rooms have central heating, phone, TV, minibar

Facilities dining-room, lobby
Credit cards AE, DC, MC, V
Children accepted
Disabled lift/elevator
Pets not accepted
Closed Dec
Manager José Vázquez

Asturias

Country hotel, Tox

Villa Borinquen

This delightful hotel could not be more secluded – even the village of Tox does not appear on most maps (look for Villapedre). Between the main coast road and the shore, the Villa Borinquen sits quietly, unsignposted, amid rolling green cultivated land, far from any distractions.

It is a modern building, based on the houses of the wealthy Spaniards who returned from the Americas in the heyday of Spanish colonialism, and everything has been put together with comfort in mind. The bedrooms are enormous, and some have huge balconies overlooking the countryside and the extensive gardens to the sea. They are all carefully and individually furnished with large beds, comfortable armchairs, long drapes at the windows and rugs on the polished wood floors.

The hotel provides breakfast and snack meals, and the same management runs a restaurant down the road at the pretty little village of Puerto Vega, which has something of the atmosphere of a Cornish fishing village. Fish and shellfish are unloaded straight into the kitchen; you can watch the harbour at work as you eat and take a stroll along the sea wall as the sun goes down.

Nearby Barayo beach (5 km); the dramatic Navia valley (10 km).

Tox, , Villapedre, Asturias
Tel (98) 5648220
Fax (98) 5648222
Location in open fields near village, 1 km N of N634, about 11 km W of Luarca; with grounds and car parking
Meals breakfast
Prices rooms PP-PPPP; breakfast P
Rooms 7 double, 1 single, 3 family rooms, all with bath; all rooms have central heating, phone, TV, minibar, hairdrier
Facilities sitting-room, breakfast-room, bar; mountain bikes
Credit cards MC, V
Children welcome; games available
Disabled access easy; lift/elevator
Pets not accepted
Closed Jan
Manager Elisa Méndez

Asturias

Historic town hotel, Salas

Castillo de Valdés-Salas

The market town of Salas is off the busy and tortuously winding road between Oviedo and the coast, in the foothills of the Cordillera Cantabrica. The town's 16thC castle has been restored and converted into a small and simple hotel, keeping much of the character of the original building intact

The massive doors lead you through the thick walls into the reception area, which also houses the local tourist information desk (both offering good spoken English). The building is constructed around a paved courtyard, with covered cloisters to shelter you from the mountain rain and from the summer sun. On the ground floor, off this patio area, is the cafeteria/restaurant, whch is open to the public and serves unfussy dishes with local touches – try their cakes made with rice, milk and sugar, served with freshly brewed coffee. The bedrooms are mostly on the first floor and are very plain but stylish, with shutters at the windows, wooden floors and modern bathrooms tiled in red and white. There are two sitting-rooms upstairs; one has a television, games and books, and both have open fires in the winter. All the windows are double-glazed too, so it should be snug.

Nearby Benedictine monastery of San Salvador, Cornellana (10 km); viewpoint at Tineo (24 km).

Plaza de la Campa, s/n, 33860, Salas, Asturias
Tel (98) 6832222
Location in village just off N634, about 45 km W of Oviedo; with garden and car parking in square
Meals breakfast, lunch, dinner
Prices rooms PP; breakfast P; meals P-PP
Rooms 12 double, all with bath; all rooms have central heating, phone

Facilities dining-room, 2 sitting-rooms, bar, terrace
Credit cards AE, MC, V
Children accepted
Disabled access difficult
Pets not accepted
Closed Jan
Proprietor Manuel López

Asturias

Town hotel, Llanes

Hotel Don Paco

The most startling feature of this hotel is the restaurant, which occupies the huge arched and vaulted hall of the original 17thC palace that forms the basis of the present-day building. It is truly impressive, with stone pilasters, an ancient polished wood floor and splendid chandeliers, and a mezzanine area from where you can survey the other diners. Local specialities include a spiny lobster which is caught in pots off the coast. Double doors lead out on to the terrace which is above the level of the pavement, beneath pollarded plane trees and shrubs sheltering the tables from the sun and the passers-by. From here you can admire the handsome stone façade of the palace as you take your coffee or aperitif.

The rest of the hotel is rather dull in comparison, and showing signs of wear, but many of the old-fashioned bedrooms look out over the quiet square or the back of the building away from the traffic. The town itself is full of bustle and interesting shops, as well as the remains of its defensive walls and castle. There are plenty of beaches nearby and the grand Picos de Europa with their rivers and mountains are within easy reach.

Nearby Monasterio de S. Antolin (10 km); Peña Tú (5 km) – megalith with engravings.

Posada Herrera 1, 33500, Llanes, Asturias
Tel (985) 400150
Location in heart of town; with some car parking
Meals breakfast, lunch, dinner
Prices rooms PP; breakfast P; meals PP
Rooms 38 double, 36 with bath, 2 with shower; 4 single with shower; all rooms have central heating, phone, TV
Facilities dining-room, sitting-room, bar
Credit cards AE, DC, MC, V
Children accepted
Disabled lift/elevator; some ground-floor rooms
Pets not accepted
Closed 1 Oct to 1 Jun
Manager Alfredo Sanpedro

Asturias

Beach hotel, Barro, Llanes

Kaype

Situated on the beautiful sandy Barro beach, this is a functional and friendly place for a seaside or mountain walking holiday: the Picos de Europa are not far inland. All the rooms have a view of either the sea or the mountains. A semi-covered terrace extends from the dining area, an agreeable place in which to chat or to read on days when there is no *orbayu*, the persistent but essential rain from the north. Unusually, the hotel has its own shellfish nurseries which supply its restaurant.

Obliging and generous, the staff have managed to build up a loyal clientele that returns year after year to the same rooms.

Nearby Torimbia beach (2 km); Llanes (6 km); Picos de Europa and Covadonga National Park (42 km).

Playa de Barro s/n, 33500, Llanes, Asturias
Tel (98) 5400904
Location on the beach; car parking
Meals breakfast, lunch, dinner
Prices rooms PP; breakfast P; meals PP
Rooms 48 double, all with bath; all rooms have central heating, telephone
Facilities sitting-room, bar, dining-room; terrace
Credit cards AE, DC, MC, V
Children welcome
Disabled all rooms equipped; lift/elevator
Pets not accepted
Closed Oct to Apr
Manager José Manuel González

Town hotel, Llanes

Paraíso

This large house with prominent tiers of bay windows was tastefully renovated a few years ago as a hotel-cum-summer apartment block for families and the occasional itinerant film star. The interior decoration, it has to be said, with its white marbles, mahogany walls and antique furniture, seems a little kitsch and decadent. Another shortcoming is noise at night from the street below. Otherwise, the hotel is impeccable. The owner, Antonio Ampudia, does not skimp. An old-fashioned Buttons greets you at the door. From your bedroom an intercom links you directly to a valet waiting to attend your every need: whether it be a snack, a baby-sitter or today's paper, you only have to ask.

Nearby the idol of Peña-Tú; Vidiago (5 km); Toró beach (1 km).

Pidal, 2, 33500, Llanes, Asturias
Tel (98) 5401784
Location in the main street of the town, next to the harbour; garage nearby
Meals breakfast
Prices rooms PP-PPPP; breakfast P
Rooms 22 double, 12 suites, all with bath; all rooms have air conditioning,
telephone, minibar, radio, TV (satellite), safe
Facilities sitting-room, cafeteria
Credit cards AE, DC, MC, V
Children welcome
Disabled no special facilities; lift/elevator
Pets not accepted
Closed Nov to Mar
Proprietor Antonio Ampudia

Asturias

Palacete Peñalba

This extraordinary house was built in 1912 by a disciple of the celebrated Spanish architect Antonio Gaudí. Everything about it – the curved sweep of the entrance steps, the ovals of the balconies, the glazed and tiled atrium, the twin towers with their delicate plasterwork, the arched alcoves in the bedrooms – is redolent of the early Art Nouveau movement which took root in Europe at this time. Much of the original furniture and internal decoration, such as the tapestries, has been preserved, and the whole edifice has been declared a National Artistic Monument. In fact, the atmosphere does rather resemble that of a museum – beware the elegant but delicate chairs in the sitting-room. This is not a place to bring unruly children, but if you enjoy the absurdities of this particular era you will come anyway.

The town of Figueras del Mar has been by-passed by the new bridge over the Ria de Ribadeo, but it is busy with fishing and shipbuilding. The hotel's owners also run a restaurant on the waterfront, and both establishments have a reputation in the area for interesting cuisine – specializing, needless to say, in seafood.

Nearby Castropol (5 km); beach and lighthouse at Tapia de Casariego (10 km).

El Cotarelo s/n,
33794, Figueras, Asturias
Tel (98) 5636125
Fax (98) 5636247
Location at top of town above port; with grounds and car parking
Meals breakfast
Prices rooms PP-PPP; breakfast P
Rooms 12 double, 2 suites, all with bath; all rooms have central heating, radio, TV, minibar, phone, safe
Facilities dining-room, sitting-room, bar
Credit cards AE, V
Children welcome
Disabled access difficult
Pets not accepted
Closed never
Proprietor Avelino Gutierrez

Asturias

Seaside hotel, Ribadesella

Hotel Ribadesella Playa

Ribadesella has long been quite a stylish resort, popular with holiday-makers attracted by the port and the estuary of the river Sella, with its sandy beaches and spectacular scenery. The Hotel Ribadesella Playa, converted from one of the many old family villas which line the bay, across the river from the main town, has recently been sensitively modernized.

The hotel is right on the beach, beside a grassed promenade, free of traffic, and many of the bedrooms – smartly done up with traditional-style modern furniture – have long windows and balconies with views over the water. The restaurant is in the lower part of the house, cool and airy, with stone floors and sympathetic wooden furniture. The *carte* is long and varied, with plenty of fresh fish dishes, and there is also a menu of the day if you prefer your selection made for you.

The hotel has no pretensions to luxury, but combines comfortable accommodation with a relaxed and informal atmosphere. A happy choice for a beach holiday, with the added advantage for many visitors of the nearby town and the mountains with their walks, caves and birdlife.

Nearby Caves of Tito Bustillo (5 km); Mirador de la Reina (45 km).

Ricardo Cangas, 3,
33560, Ribadesella, Asturias
Tel (98) 5860715
Fax (98) 5860220
Location in quiet residential beach area on W side of town; car parking in courtyard
Meals breakfast, lunch, dinner
Prices rooms PP; breakfast P; meals PP
Rooms 16 double, 1 single, all with bath; all rooms have central heating, phone, TV

Facilities dining-room, 2 sitting-rooms
Credit cards AE, DC, MC, V
Children accepted
Disabled no special facilities
Pets not accepted
Closed never
Manager José Luis García

Asturias

Mountain hotel, Besnes

La Tahona

Driving from Panes up into the Picos de Europa, you follow the course of the Rio Cares, up through a deep and dramatic gorge which winds on towards some of the most stupendous views to be found in these mountains. La Tahona is tucked away behind the tiny village of Besnes, at the end of a cobbled track, beside a stream which runs down through beech woods. It is a peaceful and simple base for walking, horseriding, down-river canoeing or mountain-biking.

The bar by the entrance hall is used by a few local farmers who drop in for a quiet coffee and brandy on their way up and down the valley; beyond is the rustic restaurant, all bare stone, exposed beams, whitewashed rough plaster and red tiles. Bedrooms are similarly simple but stylish, with tiled or wooden floors.

The stream runs past the restaurant, the terrace and the windows of the bedrooms – the soothing sound of water and birdsong will be your only distractions while contemplating the choice between salmon with cider, trout from the river or Asturian hotpot.

Nearby El Buxu – prehistoric cave paintings (30 km); viewpoint at Las Estazadas (8 km).

33578, Besnes-Alles, Asturias
Tel & fax (98) 5415749
Location in quiet wooded valley, off C6312 10 km W of Panes; with garden and car parking
Meals breakfast, lunch, dinner
Prices rooms PP; breakfast P; meals PP
Rooms 18 double, one family room, all with bath; all rooms have central heating, TV, phone

Facilities dining-room, sitting-room; horse-riding, mountain bikes, fishing, canoeing
Credit cards MC, V
Children welcome; play-room; special menus
Disabled access easy; some ground-floor rooms
Pets not accepted
Closed never
Manager Lorenzo and Sarah Nilsson

Asturias

La Casona de Mestas

To reach this mountain hideaway you follow the sinuous course of the Ponga river to the regional capital of San Juan de Beleño, passing below sheer rocky hillsides and climbing over beautiful passes. The hotel – another Rural Tourism Centre – is at the heart of some of the most spectacular walking country you could hope to find anywhere, with several well known routes starting at the Casona itself. The main building has been converted from an old house with overhanging, Alpine-style roofs, and the restaurant area is a sympathetic modern, wooden glass-sided extension looking out on to fabulous views of the surrounding peaks.

Nearby Desfiladero de los Beyos (25 km); thermal baths .

Las Mestas 33557, Ponga, Asturias
Tel (98) 5843055
Location in mountainous countryside near village, about 30 km S of Cangas de Onís; with car parking
Meals breakfast, lunch, dinner
Prices rooms PP; breakfast P; meals PP
Rooms 6 double, 6 single all with bath; all rooms have central heating
Facilities dining-room, cafeteria, TV room
Credit cards V
Children accepted
Disabled no special facilities
Pets not accepted
Closed mid-Jan to mid- Feb
Manager Vicente Cosío

La Rectoral

This was the first of the Rural Tourism hotels to be encouraged by the government of Asturias – a lovely old 18thC stone house converted into simple but comfortable accommodation reflecting the architectural, decorative and gastronomic traditions of the region. It is on the western side of Asturias, on the border with Lugo, in the remote hilly country of Los Oscos. The Rectoral looks out over unspoiled countryside which is still quietly tilled using locally made tools. Six of the bedrooms have their own lounge and private terrace, sharing the peaceful view with the hotel's patio.

Nearby Monastery, Villanueva de Oscos (20 km).

33775, Taramundi, Asturias
Tel (98) 5634060
Location on a hill, going up from the main square of the village, in front of the town hall; garden, covered car parking
Meals breakfast, lunch, dinner
Prices rooms PPP; breakfast P; meals PP
Rooms 12 double, all with bath; all rooms have central heating, air-conditioning, phone, TV, radio, minibar
Facilities dining-room, sitting-rooms, TV room, cafeteria, sauna, gymnasium
Credit cards AE, MC, V
Children accepted
Disabled no special facilities
Pets not accepted
Closed never
Manager Jesus Manuel Mier

Asturias

La Casona de Amandi

Rodrigo Fernández and his wife María Isabel Armero bought this old colonial mansion on the outskirts of Villaviciosa with the idea of turning it into a secluded country hotel in the heart of the magnificent Asturias. Close by is Ría de Villaviciosa, famous for its rich birdlife.

The proprietors' good taste, and former profession as antique dealers, is reflected in every corner: from the façade with traditional bay windows, to the Elizabethan furniture and the French garden full of hydrangeas and magnolias. This is a peaceful retreat, very much a village house, smelling of wood and mown grass.

The rooms preserve their old fittings: there are authentic washbasins and shaving bowls in some of the bathrooms. Elsewhere there are similar details: grandmother's pianola, for instance, in the sitting room. On the other hand, there is no lack of modern comfort.

The welcome is sincere and personal; Rodrigo and María live on the premises. An outstanding base from which to make forays into 'Green Spain'.

Nearby Ría de Villaviciosa (5 km); Rodiles beach (10 km); Tazones fishing harbour (10 km).

Amandi, 33300, Villaviciosa, Asturias
Tel (98) 5890130
Location on a narrow lane, 1 km from Villaviciosa; with garden and car parking
Meals breakfast
Prices rooms PPP; breakfast P
Rooms 8 double, 1 single, all with bath; all rooms have central heating, telephone, TV
Facilities sitting-room/library

Credit cards MC, V
Children welcome
Disabled access difficult
Animals not accepted
Closed never
Proprietors Rodrigo Fernández and María Isabel Armero

Pontevedra

Mansion Parador, Cambados

PT del Albariño

Cambados is a happy little holiday town which is at its best in the summer months, a judgement equally applicable to the Parador, which can be bleak and cold in winter (like any hotel in an abandoned seaside town in the off-season).

The hotel is built around a courtyard garden with palm trees and a fountain, and for anyone in vacation mood it offers cool and relaxed accommodation, right beside the protected estuary of the Ría de Arousa, with its islands and wooded banks. The water here is not as clean as Atlantic water would be, but this does not seem to deter local bathers.

There are several interesting bars and restaurants in the town with its peaceful, shady squares and long tree-lined promenade if you decide not to eat in the rather predictable Parador diningroom. Inevitably the specialities of this area are fish and shellfish, but most menus offer meat dishes too. The wines of the west coast can be delicious, particularly some of the young green wines, known locally as *joven* – the Parador itself is named after a wine brought to the area by Benedictine monks in the twelfth century.

Nearby Plaza de Fefiñanes; Monastery of Armenteira (10 km); island of La Toja (10 km).

Paseo de Cervantes s/n, 36630, Cambados, Pontevedra
Tel (986) 542250
Location in lovely gardens at north end of promenade; with car parking
Meals breakfast, lunch, dinner
Prices rooms PPP-PPPP; breakfast P; dinner PP
Rooms 51 double, 12 single, all with bath; all rooms have central heating, phone TV, safe

Facilities dining-room, sitting-room, bar, swimming-pool
Credit cards AE, DC, MC, V
Children welcome
Disabled some ground-floor rooms
Pets not accepted
Closed never
Manager Carlos Herrero

Pontevedra

Country hotel, Villagarcía de Arosa

Hotel Pazo O'Rial

The road here runs along beside the Ría de Arosa as it opens out towards the sea, not quite the open Atlantic, but nevertheless a holiday area for many Spanish visitors as well as northern Europeans.

This lovely old manor house is set back from the coast in its own gardens and has been beautifully converted, making full use of all the usual traditional effects – wooden beams, tiled floors and bare stone walls. The whole effect is softened with deep cushioned sofas, lacy curtains and woollen rugs. The service has been criticised as slack (and certainly the desk clerk was rather slow) but there is nothing amiss with the housekeeping, the gardening or the cleanliness of the pool, which is surrounded by a protective hedge on one side and lovely views over the countryside on the other.

This is another area famous for its seafood – the bays around here are packed with fish and shellfish farms, and every inlet seems to have its little fleet of fishing boats to win a share of the harvest. The menu of the hotel reflects this, with the ubiquitous grilled prawns coming high on the list along with huge mussels in a thick tomato sauce.

Nearby Vista Alegre Convent; Mirador de Lobeira (5 km).

El Rial No 1, 36600, Villagarcía de Arosa, Pontevedra
Tel (986) 507011
Fax (986) 501676
Location near sea, set back from road; with car parking
Meals breakfast, lunch, dinner
Prices rooms PP; breakfast P; meals PP
Rooms 49 double, 6 single, 4 suites, one family room; all with bath; all rooms have central heating, phone, TV
Facilities dining-room, sitting-room, bar
Credit cards AE, DC, MC, V
Children welcome
Disabled access easy; ground-floor rooms; lift/elevator
Pets not accepted
Closed never
Manager Julio Mondragón

Pontevedra

Hotel Pazo El Revel

Back from the coast road and the small town of Villalonga, up a lane which leads to walks in the hills, a little church and the local cemetery, this lovely 17thC *pazo* is the family home of Luis Ansorena Garret, an aristocratic gentleman who has run this hotel along his own lines since the 1960s.

The creeper-covered façade has no noticeboard or sign to give the hotel away. You park across the lane and help will be at hand to carry your bags through the archway to the courtyard and your neat, tiled room. Swallows nest in the age-old beams and eaves of the house and verandas, while quiet men rake the gravel and tend the beautiful formal gardens and lawns.

In the heat of summer, nothing could be more calming than to take your iced *fino* to the colonnaded terrace overlooking the trees and flowers and to sit in a padded wicker armchair for an hour or so before dinner. The dining-room is quite informal and – please note – is open only at the height of the season; but lazy breakfasts can be enjoyed into the late morning, making the most of the excellent fresh coffee and newly baked rolls, croissants and sweet cakes.

Nearby Cambados – *pazos* and restaurants (10 km); beaches at San Vicente do Mar (5 km).

Camino de la Iglesia s/n, 36990, Villalonga, Pontevedra
Tel (986) 743000
Location a short way up hill overlooking town; with gardens and car parking
Meals breakfast, lunch, dinner
Prices rooms PP-PPP; breakfast P; meals PP
Rooms 20 double, 2 single, all with bath; all rooms have central heating, phone
Facilities dining-room, sitting-room, bar, terrace; tennis court, swimming-pool
Credit cards MC, V
Children tolerated
Disabled access difficult
Pets not accepted
Closed Oct to May
Proprietor Luis Ansorena

Pontevedra

PT Casa del Barón

The approach to Pontevedra is not promising: the roads are extremely busy and smoke belches from a cement works. But, as so often in Spain, as soon as you turn into the old town, you are suddenly immersed in another world, with cobbled streets and shutters, balconies and stone façades which tell of a different way of life.

The Parador is at the heart of Pontevedra's old town, and is one of the most captivating of the chain, occupying a beautiful old *pazo* which has been the home of many grandees. It is not imposing, but rather elegant, with plenty of antiques which are meant to be used rather than just admired, giving you the feeling that this is a place where you should know how to behave –the suites in the sitting-rooms are covered in apricot-coloured suede, for example.

The dining-room is hung with tapestries and chandeliers, gilt mirrors and paintings, and overlooks the terraced garden with its fountain and rosebeds. As with many of the Paradores there are regional dishes on the menu and at the Casa del Barón this may include *lamprea* (lamprey), which can be very rich and is something of an acquired taste.

Nearby Museo Provincial; Mirador de Coto Redondo (15 km).

Calle Maceda s/n,
36002, Pontevedra
Tel (986) 855800
Fax (986) 852195
Location on cobbled street in heart of old town; with garden and car parking in courtyard
Meals breakfast, lunch, dinner
Prices rooms PP-PPP breakfast P; dinner PP
Rooms 44 double, 3 single, all with bath; all rooms have central heating, phone,
TV, minibar
Facilities dining-room, 2 sitting-rooms, bar, conference room
Credit cards AE, DC, MC, V
Children welcome
Disabled lift/elevator
Pets not accepted
Closed never
Manager José Basso

Orense

Modern hilltop Parador, Verín

PT Monterrey

The 'Monterrey' Parador is named after the dramatic castle which occupies a neighbouring hilltop, and which you can see for many miles before you reach the town of Verín. Parts of the castle church date back to the 13th century and there are towers from the 16th and 17th centuries. The whole complex was abandoned around a hundred years ago but the fortifications are now undergoing restoration.

In contrast, the Parador is a relatively recent construction, though it has been built in local stone with concessions to regional architectural style and it sits happily on its own hilltop surrounded by trees and lawns. As Paradores go it is undistinguished and is scarcely a place to spend the whole of your holidays, but the swimming-pool, the breezy setting and the nearby sights make it worthy of a short stopover.

The old town of Verín itself is quiet and picturesque, and the valley of the Támega river which runs off north from here is lined with vineyards. Wines from nearby which appear on the Parador list and which are worth trying include the lovely fruity whites from Ribeiro.

Nearby Mineral water spas at Sousas, Cabreiroa and Villaza, and bottling factory at Fontenova (5 km).

32600, Verín, Orense
Tel (988) 410075
Fax (988) 412017
Location on hill above town; with garden and car parking
Meals breakfast, lunch, dinner
Prices rooms PP-PPP; breakfast P; meals PP
Rooms rooms 22 double, one single, all with bath; all rooms have central heating, phone, TV, minibar
Facilities dining-room, sitting-room, bar, terrace; swimming-pool
Credit cards AE, DC, MC, V
Children accepted
Disabled some ground-floor bedrooms
Pets not accepted
Closed never
Manager Jesús Santamaría

Orense

Town hotel, Puebla de Trives

Pazo Casa Grande

Pazo Casa Grande is a noble 18thC stone mansion clustered around a solid central tower, crowned by a coat of arms showing a knight on horseback killing a dragon. For many years the house lay in a state of disrepair until the Alvarez family decided to renovate it in the late 1980s and open it as a *pousada*, or little hotel.

From the outside, the Casa Grande appears to be an imposing, aristocratic residence; but inside its thick walls all is elegant, cosy and welcoming. It is furnished and decorated with antiques:and Limoges ceramics, and original watercolours adorn the walls. The 18thC piano is a decoration: Doña Adelaida now prefers a modern instrument. Like any self-respecting big house, Pazo Casa Grande has its own chapel which every year, on the feast of Corpus Christi, is decorated with a carpet of flowers.

Outside, there is a delightful garden with fruit trees and a copse of chestnuts. This is a popular base from which to follow the Route of the Monasteries (Ribera Sagrada), also the Romanesque Route, and in winter for skiing.

Nearby Montefurado reservoir (6 km); Montaña Manzaneda ski resort (16 km); San Esteban de Ribas de Sil Monastery and gorges of the River Sil (60 km).

Marqués de Trives 17, 32780, Poboa de Trives, Orense
Tel & fax (988) 332066
Location in a main street of the town; garden and car parking
Meals breakfast
Prices rooms PP; breakfast P
Rooms 7 double, with bath; all rooms have central heating, TV
Facilities dining-room,
TV room, chapel
Credit cards AE, DC, MC, V
Children welcome; play area
Disabled access difficult
Pets accepted, outside the house; kennels (1km)
Closed never
Proprietor Adelaida Alvarez

León

Hostal El Palacio

For the last 25 years the Eguens have devotedly run this welcoming but little-known hotel which specializes in excellent, wholesome home cooking and cider.

As an Asturian, José Manuel Eguen knows practically everything there is to know about the bottle. In the old stables at the back he has built himself a *sidrería* – a bar – out of black wood seasoned with the smell of cider. It is also a fascinating folk museum; on the walls you will find a prehistoric one-way telephone and an ancient precursor of the Thermos flask.

The house is probably the oldest in the village, certainly the only one bearing a coat of arms. King Felipe III is supposed to have stopped off here once upon a time and seduced the mistress of the house; there is a framed document in the hall to prove it. The patio – shaded by Virginia creeper and vines – has an old cart in one corner, painted bright red and green, and a five-foot-long blacksmith's bellows in another. A cool and attractive alternative to the dining-room and sitting-room, it is looked down upon by a wide iron-railinged balcony on the first floor: both are pleasant places to sit. The rooms are light, cheerful and spotlessly clean; prepared, perhaps, more with love than taste.

Nearby Castle; León (30 km); San Miguel de Escalada (45 km).

Calle Palacio 3, 24200,
Valencia de Don Juan, León
Tel (987) 750474
Location in centre of town;
car parking in street
Meals breakfast, lunch, dinner
Prices rooms P-PP (half-price
for children); breakfast P;
dinner P
Rooms 7 double, 3 single, all
with bath; all rooms have TV
Facilities dining-room,
sitting-room, bar, patio

Credit cards not accepted
Children welcome
Disabled access difficult
Pets not accepted
Closed 1 Oct to 1 May
Proprietor José Manuel Eguen

León

Hotel Villegas II

Villegas II looks and sometimes feels more like a private house in its own grounds than a hotel. You might even drive past it, as we did, without noticing the blue hotel plaque by the door. From its external appearance you would expect the hotel to be pleasant and home-like inside, and it does not disappoint. The entrance hall is dominated by blue tiles and light wrought iron, and lit by a stained glass skylight. Neo-Arabic arches lead to the bar, dining-room and a small lounge.

All of the bedrooms give on to the garden. They have been decorated with some flair; the bedspreads and curtains are white-and-blue flowered, much of the furniture is of light wood and the doors and door-frames are of stripped pine.

Outside, there is a fringe of garden all round the building, which takes in a swimming-pool and an outdoor dining-terrace.

This hotel is everything that the Palacio (see separate entry) over the road is not. Here you can choose between two facing hotels – both charming in different ways. (Villegas I, by the way, is something else again: a modern multi-storey block down the road.)

Nearby Castle (short walk); León (30 km); San Miguel de Escalada (45 km); Astorga (55 km).

Calle Palacio 17, 24200, Valencia de Don Juan, León
Tel (987) 750161
Location in centre of town; with garden and car parking
Meals breakfast, lunch, dinner
Prices rooms PP; breakfast P; lunch PP, dinner PP
Rooms 4 double, one family room, all with bath; all rooms have central heating, TV
Facilities dining-room, sitting-room, bar, terrace; swimming-pool
Credit cards AE, DC, MC, V
Children welcome; garden play area
Disabled access difficult
Pets not accepted
Closed Dec to Feb
Proprietor Felisa Garcia

León

Hotel Gaudí

The Hotel Gaudí is right in the middle of Astorga, on the main square which has seen the meeting of Roman roads, the passing of pilgrims on their way to Santiago, and the building of the extraordinary Episcopal Palace. The Hotel takes its name from the Barcelona architect, Antonio Gaudí, who built this wildly decorated pastiche of a Gothic palace in 1889. It now houses a museum about the pilgrim ways to Santiago de Compostela.

This stylish, recently built hotel offers comforts far removed from the sort of conditions those earlier travellers would have encountered. The elegant restaurant, with its marble floor, chandeliers and panelled walls, overlooks the square – as does the bar area, which serves excellent *tapas*. Many of the bedrooms have balconies, their shutters opening on to views of the huge and complicated cathedral, with its flying buttresses and carvings, the Gaudí palace and the surrounding terracotta roofs above narrow, cobbled lanes. They are individually furnished and most are carpeted, which makes a pleasantly soft change after the bare boards and marble floors of so many Spanish hotels.

The quiet square is mostly used as a car park and is bordered by trees, shrubs and flowers, cafés and shops.

Nearby León (40 km).

Plaza Eduardo de Castro 6, 24700, Astorga, León
Tel (987) 615654
Fax (987) 615040
Location in main square near cathedral and Gaudí palace; with car parking in square
Meals breakfast, lunch, dinner
Prices rooms PP-PPP; breakfast P; meals PP
Rooms 35 double, 3 suites, all with bath; all rooms have central heating, phone, TV, radio

Facilities dining-room, sitting-room, bar
Credit cards AE, DC, MC, V
Children accepted
Disabled access difficult
Pets not accepted
Closed never
Proprietor Gaspar Ramos

Cantabria

Mountain hotel, Cosgaya

Hotel del Oso

You will already have come through some exceptional scenery to reach Cosgaya, climbing steadily all the way from the coast, and once you arrive you are surrounded by peaks, many snow- covered until early summer.

A small bridge over a clear mountain stream takes you into the forecourt of this stone-built hotel, with its wooden balconies, arched veranda and overflowing flowerpots. The public rooms are cool and dark in the summer heat, but cosy and welcoming in the winter, with log fires in the sitting-room. Although the hotel has only recently been built, it is traditional in style with plenty of workmanship to admire, in wood, terracotta tiling and bare stonework. The restaurant, too, makes use of regional specialities – fresh river trout, interesting local cheeses and regional spirits.

There is always the chance of getting snowed in when staying in this area, so bring plenty of books – it has been known to happen in June, though at that time of year you are more likely to be lazing around their pool, playing tennis or off hiking in the hills. They are used to British visitors here, and good English is spoken at the desk.

Nearby Cable-car at Fuente De (10 km) to 1800 m.

39539, Cosgaya, Cantabria
Tel (942) 733018
Fax (942) 733036
Location by stream in mountains; with garden and car parking
Meals breakfast, lunch, dinner
Prices rooms PP; breakfast P; dinner PP
Rooms 32 double, 4 single, all with bath; all rooms have central heating, phone, TV
Facilities dining-room, 3 sitting-rooms, bar; swimming-pool, tennis court
Credit cards DC, MC, V
Children welcome
Disabled access difficult
Pets not accepted
Closed 15 Jan to 15 Feb
Proprietor Severo Rivas

Cantabria

Historic Parador, Santillana del Mar

PT Gil Blas

On a fleeting visit, Santillana can seem like an overpopulated film set, but if you stay overnight you will have opportunity and time to take in the essence of the place. The Parador Gil Blas – one of the most captivating of the Paradores – is without doubt the place to stay if you have the choice.

Gil Blas was the fictional hero of a story by the French writer Lesage, a fact seemingly unconnected with the house itself, which was the country home of the Barreda Bracho family, built in the 15th and 16th centuries. The worn stone, the lovely terracotta roof tiles, the delightful courtyard garden and the cobbled entrance hall are all in harmony with the medieval atmosphere of the village.

There are two parts to this Parador – the original fine old manor house right in the centre of Santillana del Mar, and the new annexe across the square. It would not be a complete disaster if you ended up with a new room, but the character of Gil Blas is something special and the rooms are exceptional; many have long windows and balconies but the ones overlooking the garden are probably the most pleasant.

Nearby Villas House, Calle de Santo Domingo; Velarde Tower, Plaza de Las Arenas; Altamira cave exhibition (5 km).

Plaza Ramón Pelayo 11, 39330, Santillana del Mar, Cantabria
Tel (942) 818000
Location on main square in heart of village; with garden and garage
Meals breakfast, lunch, dinner
Prices rooms PP-PPPP; breakfast P; meals PP
Rooms 51 double, 4 single; all rooms have central heating, phone, TV, minibar, safe
Facilities dining-room, 3 sitting-rooms, breakfast room, sauna, bar, conference room
Credit cards AE, DC, MC, V
Children accepted
Disabled no special facilities
Pets not accepted
Closed never
Manager Cesar Alvarez Montoto

Cantabria

Village hotel, Santillana del Mar

Hotel Altamira

If you want to be right in the heart of the old village of Santillana del Mar, in an old house which has retained much of its character whilst offering full facilities, but you have had enough of Paradores, then the Hotel Altamira will probably suit you.

The hotel was extended to take in the house next door, and has a large courtyard garden at the back which doubles as a terrace for outside dining or drinking when the weather is right. The place has a comfortable air of antiquity, with old chests, chairs, paintings and mirrors dotted around, but is not at all like a museum.

The restaurant is in country style, with red and white cloths and tiled floors, the breakfast room quiet, dark and green, under lovely stone arches. The wooden stairs – pleasantly creaky, with nicely old-fashioned flowered carpet – lead from the stone-flagged entrance hall up to the sitting-rooms and bedrooms which are found off at interesting angles and on different levels. The bedrooms themselves are furnished in keeping with the atmosphere of the house, with its polished wood floors, beams and, in places, bare stone walls.

Nearby Villas House, Calle de Santo Domingo; Velarde Tower, Plaza de Las Arenas; Altamira cave exhibition (5 km).

Cantón 1, 39330, Santillana del Mar, Cantabria
Tel (942) 818025
Fax (942) 840136
Location in old village, on road to church; no private car parking, but municipal car park nearby
Meals breakfast, lunch, dinner
Prices rooms PP-PPP; breakfast P; meals PP
Rooms 19 double, 5 single, 2 suites, 6 family rooms, all with bath; all rooms have central heating, phone, TV, hairdrier
Facilities 2 dining-rooms, 1 sitting-room, bar, terrace, café
Credit cards AE, DC, MC, V
Children accepted
Disabled access difficult
Pets not accepted
Closed 24 Dec and 31 Jan
Manager David Oceja

Cantabria

Village hotel, Santillana del Mar

Los Infantes

The Hotel Los Infantes, set slightly back from the main road, just outside the village of Santillana del Mar, has been built around a lovely old 18thC stone country house. Entering the hall from the terrace through a decorated stone archway you can sense the grandeur of the old ways of life. There are huge carved chests on stone floors, wrought iron chandeliers hanging from high ceilings with massive wooden beams, and an impressive collection of antique clocks. The bar is in the lobby area, and you can sink into a deep leather armchair and soak up the atmosphere here or take your drink out into the sheltered garden. The upstairs sitting-room also has leather armchairs, as well as more formal reproduction furniture.

The restaurant is modern and unfussy, in café style. Some of the bedrooms are rather undistinguished, with small bathrooms; others are individually furnished with antique bed-heads, paintings on the walls, white handwoven bedspreads, comfortable chairs, carpets, balconies and large, immaculate bathrooms. A few metres from the hotel is a new annexe offering 20 more bedrooms.

Nearby sights of Santillana del Mar; Altamira cave exhibition (1.5 km).

Avenida Le Dorat 1, 39330, Santillana del Mar, Cantabria
Tel (942) 818100
Fax (942) 840 103
Location on main road past village, near Diocesano Museum; parking for 20 cars
Meals breakfast, lunch, dinner
Prices rooms PP-PPPP; breakfast P; meals PP
Rooms 25 double, 3 single, 2 suites, all with bath; all rooms have central heating, phone, TV
Facilities dining-room, sitting-room
Credit cards AE, DC, MC, V
Children accepted
Disabled ground-floor rooms
Pets by arrangement only
Closed Oct to Apr
Proprietor Mesones Gómez

Cantabria

Posada Santa Juliana

Although the bedrooms are unpromisingly located above a souvenir shop, with their chestnut floors and oak beams, they do share some of Santillana's undiluted medieval atmosphere – especially the two in the attic.

There are no public rooms and meals are served in the bar across the street, Bodegón El Noble, where you will find the genial owner, Sr Morquilles.

The framed letter and royal shield on the souvenir shop wall explain why animals are not accepted in the posada: the Queen of Spain's dogs once stayed here but they scratched the doors.

Nearby sights of Santillana del Mar; Altamira caves (2km).

Carrera 19, 39330, Santillana del Mar, Cantabria.
Tel (942) 840106
Location in one of the main streets; car parking in street
Meals breakfast, lunch, dinner
Prices rooms P-PP, breakfast P; meals P
Rooms 8 double, all with bath; all rooms have central heating, TV
Facilities bar/restaurant

Credit cards AE, MC, V
Children accepted
Disabled access difficult
Pets not accepted
Closed never
Proprietor Carlos Morquilles

Venta de Carmona

There are few villages as unspoilt and picturesque as Carmona with its unpaved streets and stone Cantabrian houses sheltering under variegated pantiled roofs.

The largest house in the village has been turned into a hotel by the regional government. The rooms are extremely varied. All have views either over the rooftops of the village or onto the great green slopes around. Several of them are reached across the large first floor lounge. Service is impersonal and consequently atmosphere is lacking inside the hotel but for that you only have to step outside.

Nearby village; Hermida gorge (35km); Saja beechwoods (25km).

Barrio del Palacio, 39554 Carmona, Cantabria
Tel (942) 728057
Location at the top of the village
Meals breakfast, lunch, dinner
Prices rooms PP; breakfast P; meals PP
Rooms 6 double, 2 triple, all with bath; all rooms have central heating and phone
Facilities sitting-room, dining- room, bar
Credit cards V
Children accepted
Disabled access difficult
Pets not accepted
Closed mid-Jan to early Mar
Manager Teresa Martínez

Cantabria

Country house hotel, Quijas, Torrelavega

Hostería de Quijas

After several years living abroad, the Castañeda family returned home to transform this palatial 18thC house near Torrelavega into an exemplary rural hotel.

The house, with its stone walls, spreading eaves, bay windows and timbered ceilings, has been restored with great care, especially noticeable in the former library (now the reception area) and the private oratory of a former owner (approved by a bull of Pope Leon XIII).

The hotel's most outstanding feature is the 4,000 square metre garden which surrounds it on three sides with hydrangeas, climbers, and a magnolia several hundred years old, under which you can sit. The terrace is covered by a shady grapevine.

Demetrio Castañeda and his daughter Sonia serve their guests in person. The restaurant enjoys a reputation of its own: Javier Sobrón, a local chef who once cooked for the King of Spain, supervises the excellent cooking which includes too many specialities, all exquisitely presented, to list in full.

It is a shame that the main Oviedo to Santander road, with its heavy traffic, runs so close to the hotel. When booking, make sure you ask for a room on the other side.

Nearby Santillana del Mar (4 km); Altamira caves (5 km).

Barrio Vinuesa s/n, 39590, Quijas, Reocín, Cantabria
Tel (942) 820833
Fax (942) 838050
Location on the main road from Oviedo to Santander; car parking and garden
Meals breakfast, lunch, dinner
Prices rooms PP-PPPP; breakfast P; meals PPP
Rooms 12 double, one single, 6 suites, all with bath; all rooms have central heating, telephone, TV (satellite), hairdrier, minibar
Facilities sitting-room, 2 dining-rooms, bar, terrace; garden, swimming-pool
Credit cards AE, DC, MC, V
Children welcome
Disabled access difficult
Pets not accepted
Closed 23 Dec to 4 Jan
Proprietor Demetrio Castañeda

Vizcaya

Town hotel, Mundaka

Atalaya

There are no changes to report at this turn-of-the-century house, with its bright white façade dominated by bay windows, which stands close to the fishing port of Mundaka at the mouth of the Ría de Guernica. It has been decorated in an English style and transformed into a small family hotel. Extremely well kept and run, it undoubtedly provides the best accommodation on this stretch of coast.

To enter, you have to use the intercom. You will be received by the owner, Mari Carmen Alonso, or her husband. Both exude Basque honesty and hospitality. The rear hall, which serves as a cafeteria, smells of fresh bread and marmalade. An air-conditioned conservatory (without plants) has been added to act as a breakfast room and bar. Bedrooms have been very carefully put together, with every detail attended to: the magazine racks, for instance, may well contain up-to-date foreign publications. They are, however, a little small, even if the beds themselves are large.

Through the bay windows there are views of the church, the adjacent beach and the Bay of Biscay where it meets the estuary. This is a place for anyone who appreciates silence and a seemingly home-like atmosphere.

Nearby Santa María church; Guernica, Basque capital (14 km).

Paseo de Txorrokopunta, 2, 48360, Mundaka, Vizcaya
Tel (94) 6876888
Fax (94) 6876899
Location in front of the port, on the Ría de Guernica; garden and car parking
Meals breakfast
Prices PP-PPPP; breakfast P
Rooms 12 double, 2 single, one suite, all with bath; all rooms have central heating, telephone, radio, TV (satellite), minibar
Facilities dining-room, sitting-room, bar, garden
Credit cards AE, DC, MC, V
Children welcome; baby-sitting service
Disabled obliging staff to help
Pets accepted
Closed never
Proprietor Mari Carmen Alonso

Guipúzcoa

Historic palace, Hondarribia (Fuenterrabía)

Pampinot

Olga Alvarez bought this palatial house in the oldest part of historic Hondarribia with the intention of living in it herself. Only after renovating it did she have the idea to convert it into a small and uniquely personal hotel with eight cosy rooms.

The building has almost as long a history as the town, whose steep streets and ramparts are a reminder of its former importance. Before becoming a hotel, the house served variously as a warehouse, cider brewery and aristocratic residence. Maria Teresa stayed here before her wedding with Louis XIV.

With such a distinguished pedigree, it is, as you would expect, filled with antique furniture, chandeliers, plastered lintels, carpeted floors and other fine ornaments.

The bedrooms are spacious, comfortable and softly lit. The TV seems out of place, however, and the bathrooms are rather sparingly decorated. But the core of this place's appeal lies in the feminine touch, the sensitivity, and the good manners of Olga Alvarez and her team. It is unique in the region: a quintessential charming small hotel.

Nearby Castle of Carlos V, now a Parador; Jaizkíbel golf course (5 km); San Sebastian (21 km).

Mayor, 3, 20280 Hondarribia (Fuenterrabía), Guipúzcoa
Tel (943) 640600
Fax (943) 645128
Location in the main street, in the historic city centre; no car parking
Meals breakfast
Prices rooms PPP-PPPP; breakfast P
Rooms 3 double, one single, 3 family rooms, one suite, all with bath; all rooms have central heating, telephone, TV, minibar, safe
Facilities sitting-room, bar, breakfast room
Credit cards AE, DC, MC, V
Children very welcome; games and stories available
Disabled access difficult
Pets accepted
Closed Nov
Proprietor Olga Alvarez

Alava

Palace Parador, Argomániz, Vitoria

Parador de Argomániz

The Parador is reached by a narrow lane branching off from the Madrid-Irun road near Vitoria. It stands on the slopes of Mount Zabalgaña, above the few humble houses of the village, from where it commands views of the sierras of Urbasa and Gorbea, Estíbaliz monastery, the Alava plains and Vitoria. It is a stone palace, built in the 17th century by the Larrea family: austere and monumental, it reflects the origins of its owners, knights of the Order of Calatrava and ministers of Spanish monarchs. Napoleon stayed here before fighting Spanish troops at Vitoria.

The reception hall and dining-room (formerly a granary) have handsome timbered ceilings. The decorative style is distinctly Castilian – oil paintings, wall lamps, iron bolts – relieved by the antique furniture and potted plants typical of Paradors.

The rooms have bay windows, a typical local architectural feature, which make an attractive space in which to breakfast, while looking out over the green countryside. The bedroom floors and the bathrooms are arguably in need of attention. Perhaps the most memorable feature of this Parador is its silence: a place for early nights and sound sleep.

Nearby Vitoria (15 km); Estíbaliz Sanctuary (4 km); Zadorra reservoir (15 km).

Ctra. N1, km 363
01192 Argomániz, Alava
Tel (945) 293200
Tel (945) 293287
Location in a small country village; garden and car parking
Meals breakfast, lunch, dinner
Prices rooms PP-PPP; breakfast P; meals PP
Rooms 54 double, all with bath; all rooms have central heating, telephone, minibar, TV
Facilities 3 sitting-rooms, cafeteria, dining-room
Credit cards AE, DC, MC, V
Children welcome
Disabled access easy
Pets not accepted
Closed never
Manager Jorge Ridriguez

Basque country/Navarra

Hotels in San Sebastián and Pamplona

Visitors from Britain tend to overlook the Basque country just over the French border in their hurry to explore the Picos or the coastline of Galicia to the west. Yet it has a lot to offer. Not least of the attractions is the smart seaside resort of San Sebastián (or Donostia - duplicate names are a constant reminder here of the Basque separatist movement). In a region noted for fine food, this is probably the gastronomic headquarters; sadly, none of the best restaurants has rooms. Two places to stay stand out, neither of them cheap: the big and charmless Monte Igueldo, which enjoys a heart-stopping view (especially at night) from the peak of the same name at one side of the sweeping Bahía de la Concha (Tel (943) 210211); and the lovely old seafront Hotel de Londres y de Inglaterra (Tel (943) 426989), as gracious a seaside hotel as you could wish for.

Thanks largely to Hemingway's novels, Pamplona is world-famous for its July fiesta. The bulls run under the windows of the centrally-located and old-fashioned La Perla (Tel (948) 227706. Upper rooms in the more peaceful, 28-room Eslava (Tel (948) 222270) look out on the countryside beyond the city walls.

Paradores in North Central Spain

Those who arrive in Spain on the Santander ferry are in reach of three Paradores. The PT Gil Blas at Santillana del Mar (see page 45) is one of the best of the chain. The others are modern, but enjoy enviable positions in the mountains of the Picos de Europa. The otherwise dreary PT Río Deva at Fuente Dé is spectacularly set high up in a natural amphitheatre, close to a cable-car giving access to wonderful views and walks (Tel (942) 730001). PT Fuentes Carrionas is further south at Cervera de Pisuerga in the less spectacular foothills of the Picos, but is a rather more stylish hotel (Tel (988) 870075).

East and south-east of Santander are some wonderfully historic Paradores. The oldest, PT El Emperador at Fuenterrabía, is built in the remains of a 10thC fortress whose crumbling ten-foot thick walls are in constant need of restoration. It is high on our agenda for inspection for a future edition (Tel (943) 642140). The PT de Argómaniz, east of Vitoria, has 54 rooms in wings built on to a mellow 300-year-old mansion (see page 52). South of Pamplona is the PT Príncipe de Viana at Olite (medieval capital of Navarra), a fairy-tale castle of turrets and towers, with some splendid rooms within (Tel (948) 740000). The PT Marco Fabio Quintiliano at nearby Calahorra in La Rioja is a modern building of five floors with 63 rooms (Tel (941) 130358).

Navarra

Hospedería de Leyre

Situated in a landscape of exceptional beauty, this hotel is housed is one of the outbuildings of the Benedictine monastery of Leyre, which was the political and spiritual centre of the kingdom of Navarra during the 11thC.

From some of the rooms there is an unbeatable view of the valley; others overlook the old cloister, now a garden. The hotel is simple, furnished according to the needs of comfort and service. It is an ideal place to rest, to meditate or to use as a base from which to walk in the surrounding countryside. The restaurant serves typical Navarra food. If you want to sample monastic life, there are rooms (for men only) inside the monastery itself.

Nearby Foz de Lumbier gorge (4 km), Javier castle (8 km).

Monasterio de Leyre, 31410, Yesa, Navarra
Tel (948) 884100
Location on the road from Yesa reservoir; car parking
Meals breakfast, lunch, dinner
Prices rooms PP; breakfast P, meals PP
Rooms 13 double, 14 single, 5 suites, all with bath; all rooms have central heating,
phone
Facilities dining-room, bar, meeting room, TV room
Credit cards AE, DC, V
Children welcome
Disabled no special facilities
Pets not accepted
Closed mid-Dec to Mar
Manager Mercedes Casado

Méson del Peregrino

This imitation-old timber and stone building sits beside a busy main road on the ancient pilgrim route to Santiago de Compostela. It has recently been taken over by distinguished restaurateurs and the rooms – 'small and dark' criticized one reporter – are yet to be renovated.

The split level restaurant with its subdued lighting, sloping beamed ceilings and stone arches is a delight. Potted plants and collections of curios contrast with the bare stone floors and walls. Even without the improvements planned for the bedrooms this is a comfortable place for an overnight stop and a great meal.

Nearby Pilgrim's bridge 1.5km; Estella (19km); Olite (28km).

Ctra Pamplona-Logroño, km 23, Puente la Reina, Navarra
Tel (948) 340075
Location 1km from the town centre on the road from Pamplona; garden and car parking
Meals breakfast, lunch, dinner
Prices rooms PP-PPPP; breakfast P; meals PPP
Rooms 14 double, all with bath; all rooms have
telephone, TV
Facilities dining-room, bar; swimming-pool
Credit cards MC, V
Children welcome; play area
Disabled no special facilities
Pets accepted
Closed restaurant only 24 Dec to 3 Jan
Proprietor Angelo Camberro and Angelines Sedano

La Rioja

Converted monastery, Haro

Los Agustinos

In times past the famous wine growing areas of La Rioja had many monasteries and convents lodging pilgrims on the road to Santiago de Compostela. This deconsecrated Augustinian monastery in the centre of Haro still houses latter-day travellers but in more luxury than their pious predecessors.

The building, with its massively thick walls, has also been used as an arsenal, hospital, school and town prison: you can still read the graffitti, with names and dates, written by prisoners on the columns of the magnificent cloister.

Another highlight of the hotel is the sitting-room, a vast chamber crossed by great arches, containing various tapestries and a grand piano. The dining-room, bar and other public rooms, though, are non-descript. For a special room book number 124 in which the bed lies in a recess with a stone arch overhead. Otherwise the rooms are disappointingly characterless. Six of them on the second floor have views over the patio.

This is a useful centre for visiting the surrounding bodegas (wineries) which have made La Rioja famous. A major event in June is Haro's annual 'Battle of Wine'.

Nearby St Thomas's church; bodegas, vineyards and entomological centre; Bilibio crags.

San Agustin, 2, 26200, Haro, La Rioja
Tel (941) 311308
Fax (941) 303148
Location in the town centre; no car parking
Meals breakfast, lunch, dinner
Prices rooms PPP-PPPP; breakfast P; meals PP
Rooms 54 double, 6 single, 2 suites all with bath; all rooms have air-conditioning, telephone, TV (satellite) minibar, hairdrier
Facilities 4 conference rooms, sitting-room, bar, dining-room; interior cloisters
Credit cards AE, DC, V
Children welcome
Disabled access easy; lift/elevator
Pets accepted
Closed never
Proprietor Jesús de Miguel

Burgos

Roadside hotel, Burgos

Hotel Landa Palace

Forget real palaces for a moment; this is the eccentric dream of one Señora Landa. Some consider it luxurious, charmingly over-the-top or supremely pretentious; we see it as great fun. A sense of excess is aroused by the prodigious collection of old horse carts outside; but inside you are positively whisked away from reality into a Gothic fantasy. The tower you step into, transported to this convenient roadside location from a neighbouring village, is the only genuinely old part of the hotel. All the rest – including the Gothic vaults over the larger dining-room and the swimming-pool, and the carved spiral staircases – was built in the 60s.

The bedrooms are no less excessive. The grand suite has doors of polished walnut and a brass bedstead surmounted by a crown. Its sitting-room – containing a massive antique desk and five-seater settee – could house a numerous family. But don't look out of the romantic, *ajimez* window or the spell will be broken by the sight of the main Burgos-Madrid road.

There are antiques and greenery everywhere, and surprises at every turn. The corridor outside the dining-rooms ticks to the rhythm of umpteen wall clocks.

Nearby Burgos; Miraflores Carthusian Monastery (5 km).

Carretera Madrid km 235,
09000, Burgos
Tel (947) 206343
Tel (947) 264676
Location on main road to
Madrid; with garden and car
parking
Meals breakfast, lunch, dinner
Prices rooms PPPP; breakfast
PP; dinner PPP
Rooms 34 double, 3, single, 5
suites, all with bath; all rooms
have central heating,
air-conditioning, phone, TV;
most rooms have hairdrier
Facilities dining-room, 4
sitting-rooms, bar,
swimming-pool
Credit cards not accepted
Children welcome;
baby-sitting available
Disabled access difficult; lift
Pets not accepted
Closed never
Manager Francisco Javier
Revuelta

Burgos

City hotel, Burgos

Mesón del Cid

Opposite the Cathedral and on its own little square, this hotel looks like a pleasingly proportioned, much overgrown cottage. Its owner is a book-collector – most appropriate, as Burgos is a city associated with early printing – and almost the first thing that you will see inside is a reproduction of an illuminated manuscript on display in the hall. Not, as it turns out, the famous El Cid poem, which is the theme of the rest of the hotel.

Although less than ten years old, the building has been decorated with great style and sensitivity. The floors and bedrooms are named after kings, queens and other characters from El Cid. Particularly striking are the bathrooms, with out-of-the-ordinary matt porcelain basins and chunky brass taps. The bedroom furniture is antique or reproduction, with iron and brass bedsteads and some fine details such as a black-and-brass phone in one room.

Best of the public rooms is the basement bar with black chairs and marble-topped tables. The next-door disco doubles inadequately as a sitting-room. The dining-room upstairs is rectangular and low-ceilinged; there is also a separate public restaurant, connected to the hotel by a passageway, with a choice of rooms.

Nearby Cathedral; Miraflores Carthusian Monastery (4 km).

Plaza Santa Maria 8, 09003, Burgos
Tel (947) 208715
Fax (947) 269460
Location in front of cathedral in city centre; with private garage
Meals breakfast, lunch, dinner
Prices rooms PPP-PPPP; breakfast P; dinner PP
Rooms 21 double, 5 single, 3 suites, all with bath; all rooms have central heating, phone, TV, radio
Facilities dining-room, sitting-room/disco, bar
Credit cards AE, DC, MC, V
Children welcome; baby-sitting available
Disabled access easy; lift/elevator
Pets accepted
Closed never
Proprietor José López

Burgos

Village hotel, Covarrubias

Hotel Arlanza

The Arlanza takes up one side of an attractive cobbled square (closed to traffic) in a clean, prettily restored village full of half-timbered houses, shady porticoes and balconies decked with flower pots.

It is not one of those hotels brimming over with space and facilities, and is all the more refreshing for this. But, with black beams overhead and a handsome, wide, tiled staircase, it has some character. The sitting-room, unfortunately, is combined with the bar, and there is nowhere else pleasant to sit. But you will eat well in the dining-room, which is dimly lit by one small window. The Castilian soup is served so hot that it has to be eaten with a wooden spoon. Wild boar – plentiful in these parts, and a nocturnal traffic hazard until the start of the hunting season – is served in rich savoury slices.

The bedrooms, leading off dark corridors paved with squeaky red tiles, are very simply furnished. There is an occasional clash of striped and stippled marbles and the bathrooms are in need of improvement. But you get no more or less than you need for a comfortable night.

Nearby Santo Domingo de Silos and Yecla Gorge (20 km), Quintanilla de las Viñas (25 km).

Plaza de Doña Urraca, 09346, Covarrubias, Burgos
Tel (947) 406441
Fax (947) 406359
E-mail arlanza@ctv.es
Location on main square; no car parking in square
Meals breakfast, lunch, dinner
Prices rooms PP-PPP; breakfast P; dinner PP
Rooms 32 double, 2 single, 2 suites, one family room, all with bath; all rooms have central heating, phone
Facilities 2 dining-rooms, sitting-room, bar
Credit cards AE, DC, V
Children welcome
Disabled access easy; lift/elevator
Pets accepted
Closed 15 Dec to 15 Mar
Proprietor Juan José Ortiz

Burgos

Hotel Tres Coronas de Silos

A charming, peaceful establishment, so unpretentious that it doubles as the village newsagents, this is the place to come if you want to be undisturbed. You can hear the birds singing – though in high season you must wait until the coach parties go home.

The hotel is the dominant house on the village square, with a semi-circular arched doorway and a proud coat of arms over its central balcony (which belongs to room number 9, by the way). Inside, there is an overwhelming effect of renovated stone and ancient, seasoned wood (all of it skilful reproduction). Each of the rooms has at least one bare stone wall, an ample ration of solid furniture and a large, tinted mirror. Those at the front of the building look out on to the square through leaded lights fringed with stained glass.

The bar is small, frequently dominated by the TV and insufficiently lit to write in, and the only sitting-area is on the second floor landing. The dining-room includes its own wood-fired roasting oven. (But for half the price of a menu here you can get a good, although more casual, meal in the Hostal Santo Domingo de Silos, a minute's walk away, prepared and served by a delightfully jolly landlady.)

Nearby Monastery and cloister; Yecla Gorge (5 km).

Plaza Mayor 6, 09610, Santo Domingo de Silos, Burgos
Tel (947) 390047
Fax (947) 390065
Location near monastery, in main square; car parking on square
Meals breakfast, lunch, dinner
Prices rooms P-PP; breakfast P; lunch PP-PPP, dinner PP
Rooms 14 double, 2 single, all with bath; all rooms have central heating, phone

Facilities dining-room, bar
Credit cards AE, MC, V
Children welcome
Disabled access impossible
Pets not accepted
Closed never
Proprietor Emeterio Martín

Zaragoza

Former monastery, Nuévalos

Monasterio de Piedra

It is not often that you will find alabaster window panes in a hotel, but glass was not available to the seven Cistercian monks and their abbot who, in the 12th century, founded what is today one of Spain's most intriguing hotels.

The echoing, cavernous corridors – hung with signs imploring silence, and chilly in winter – might as well be time tunnels leading you back to the first millenium AD. If you know where to look, you can still see traces of the castle on top of which the monks built – machicolations and parts of the moat – breaking through centuries of masonry. Beside the cloisters there is a dank Romanesque passageway that may date from as early as the 7th century. The enormous staircase, with vaulting and fading frescoes above will leave you with a stiff neck.

The rooms are varied and were all renovated in 1997. The best of them is Room 206, on its own entresol up a private staircase. Many look out on to the beautiful park, full of rocks and waterfalls (visible from the hotel when the leaves fall in autumn), that attracts vast numbers of visitors annually; hotel guests receive a complimentary ticket for both this and the Cloisters.

The hotel is busy with adult education courses in summer.
Nearby Maluenda (40 km); scenic road to Turmiel (45 km).

50210, Nuévalos, Zaragoza
Tel (976) 849011
Location at entrance to park of same name, a few kilometres outside Nuévalos; with garden and car park
Meals breakfast, lunch, dinner
Prices rooms PP-PPPP; breakfast P; dinner PP
Rooms 44 double, 8 single, 9 family rooms, all with bath; all rooms have central heating, phone, TV, safe

Facilities sitting-room, bar, TV rooms, games room, dining-room, swimming-pool, tennis court, terrace
Credit cards AE, DC, MC, V
Children welcome
Disabled ramp access and specially adapted facilities
Pets accepted only in rooms
Closed never
Manager José María Montaner

Huesca/Lérida

Hotels in Huesca and Lérida

The provinces of Huesca and Lérida are not on the track beaten by most foreign tourists. This is not to say that they have nothing to offer the visitor, but the major attractions are the outdoor activities and scenery of the Pyrenees, the mountains forming the border with France, and rightly or wrongly these are not the usual target of non-Spanish holiday-makers. Not surprisingly, the best hotels are concentrated here; access is not easy – even by Alpine standards, the Pyrenean roads can be tortuous and slow.

The feature box on page 65 includes several mountain hotels, including the PT del Monte Perdido, just to the east of the spectacular Monte Perdido massif, which forms part of a very impressive National Park. On the other side of the Park there is simple but satisfactory accommodation to be found in and around Torla; the 70-room Ordesa is beautifully situated (Tel (974) 486125). The Paradores at Viella and Arties are mainly ski-oriented; an interesting alternative to the latter for gastronomes (but closed in early summer and early winter) is the Michelin-starred 30-room Valartiés (Tel (973) 640900). Lérida does not attract many visitors and is not notably well prepared to receive them, but Huesca is a pleasant place with some interesting sights. Best-in-town (it does not face much opposition) is the smooth 120-room Pedro I de Aragón, just outside the centre (Tel (974) 220300).

Faus-Hutte

At the foot of the 2,886-metre Mount Collarada, on the right bank of the River Aragón, sits the little town of Villanúa. Some years ago, Agustín Faus realized that this was an ideal setting for a cosy hotel offering a peaceful refuge in both winter and summer. The result is a hotel in Alpine style making much use of wood: parquet floors, panelled walls, heavy shutters and balconies on which to sit in a rocking chair and gaze at the view. Sr. Faus has seen to it that you will be warm at night beneath a feather quilt. 'Our customers are friends and they feel more at home than at home', he promises in his brochure.

Nearby Aruej Romanesque chapel; Las Guixas cave.

Ctra. de Francia, km 658.5
22870, Villanúa, Huesca
Tel (974) 378136
Location on the main road towards the Collarada; garden, car parking and garage
Meals breakfast, lunch, dinner
Prices rooms PP-PPPP; breakfast P; meals PP
Rooms 7 double, one single, one suite, one family room, all with bath; all rooms have central heating, telephone, TV
Facilities dining-room, bar; terrace; gymnasium, 2 sitting-rooms; guided trekking excursions
Credit cards AE, DC, V
Children welcome
Disabled access easy
Pets accepted
Closed never
Proprietor Agustín Faus

Huesca

Mountain hotel, Formigal

Villa de Sallent

Fidel Tejero and his family, owners of a well-known restaurant, invested all their savings in this stone and slate hotel situated at the foot of the ski slopes of Formigal, the ski resort in the Tena Valley of the Pyrenees. As you enter the hall you almost feel that you are in Switzerland or Scandinavia, rather than Spain. The wood panelling, pine furniture, the indirect lighting and the linen curtains are restful and charming.

The rooms are perfectly sealed to resist the cold. Watching the snow fall past your window while you are under a hot shower is not the least of the pleasures of this place. The bathrooms are small, however, and the bedroom walls thin.

Villa de Sallent is as comfortable for a snowed-in winter week, spent by the fireplace in the sitting-room, as for a month in summer, spent walking – walking is good not only from here but from other centres in the valley, particularly Sallent, off the C136.

There is a convenient lift to take you directly from the garage-cum-ski store to your bedroom at the end of an exhausting day's skiing. As you ascend, there is also the happy thought that Fidel is in the kitchen preparing supper.

Nearby France (6 km); Panticosa spa (21 km); Jaca (49 km).

Urbanización Formigal, 22640, Sallent de Gállego, Huesca
Tel (974) 490223
Fax (974) 490150
Location on the hill of the estate, near the church and the ski office; garage with ski store
Meals breakfast, lunch, dinner
Prices rooms PPP; breakfast P; meals PP
Rooms 36 double, 4 single, one suite, all with bath; all rooms have central heating, telephone, TV
Facilities sitting-room, bar, dining-room
Credit cards AE, DC, MC, V
Children welcome; 20% discount
Disabled lift/elevator, obliging staff
Pets not accepted
Closed never
Proprietor Fidel Tejero

Lérida

El Castell

This hotel is 10 kilometres from the border with Andorra, in the Urgellet Valley. A low-lying modern building of wood and slate, it sits snugly and unobtrusively under the castle of Seu d'Urgell. Its long line of balconies gives impressive views of the Cadí mountains.

The interior is intimate and sumptuous, but not affected. Owners Jaume Tàpies and his wife Ludi have managed to create one of the most welcoming atmospheres in the Catalan Pyrenees. They pay more than due attention to the kitchen, of which they feel especially proud and which has had some outstanding reviews. The menu includes Catalan mountain dishes (wild boar and pigs' trotters) but is also influenced by the proximity of France, evident in the exquisite *foie gras* and the interesting wine list. The dining-room has large windows opening on to the River Segre and the town of La Seu, which has a magnificent Romanesque cathedral.

A distinguished clientele, more used to grand city hotels, comes here at weekends and holidays for the peace of the mountains and the rich living. The hotel makes an excellent base for skiing or hiking in the mountains, or for shopping in Andorra.

Nearby castle; La Seu d'Urgell cathedral; Andorra (10 km); Sant Joan de l'Erm ski resort (30 km).

Ctra. de Lérida a Puigcerdà, km 129, 25700, La Seu d'Urgell, Lérida
Tel (973) 350704
Location on top of a hill with views of the valley of Urgellet; car parking and garden
Meals breakfast, lunch, dinner
Prices rooms PPP-PPPP; breakfast P; meals PPP
Rooms 34 double, 4 suites, all with bath; all rooms have air-conditioning, telephone, minibar, radio, TV (satellite), safe
Facilities dining-room, cafeteria, meeting room, terrace; swimming-pool
Credit cards AE, DC, MC, V
Children welcome
Disabled no special facilities
Pets accepted
Closed restaurant only, Jan 7 to Feb 7
Proprietor Jaume Tàpies i Travé

Lérida

Village guest house, Tremp

Casa Guilla

Britons Richard and Sandra Loder opened this ancient, labyrinthine stone farmhouse on the edge of a rock as a guest-house in 1986.

The former granaries and animal pens have become bed-rooms, part of the stables a bar, the hayloft a sitting-room-cum-library and the farmyard a terrace overlooking the two lakes of the Tremp valley from a height of 1000m.

This is still the Loders' home and although the house will take 10-15 people they prefer to keep the numbers down 'so that our guests can feel the house is theirs to come and go freely from.' On the edge of a nature reserve, Casa Guilla is popular with natu-ralists.

Guests pay for half-board with discounts for meals not taken. Everyone eats together around the same table shipboard style. 'When you have the right mix of people,' says Sandra Loder, 'everything goes fine.' If after-dinner conversation is not for you there are a TV, video and board games in the sitting-room.

The village of Santa Engràcia can be hard to find and you'd be wise to ask the Loders to send you directions in advance.

Nearby hang gliding centre (43 km); Aigues Torres National Park (80km); ski resorts (110 km); Andorra (110 km).

Santa Engràcia, Tremp 25636, Lérida **Tel & fax** (973) 252080 **Location** from Pobla de Segur take C147 towards Tremp. After 5 km turn right into Salas de Pallars, then right at school, following signs to Santa Engràcia; house is near church, 10 km from Salas; car parking **Meals** breakfast, snack lunch, dinner	**Prices** bed, breakfast and evening meal P; snack lunch P **Rooms** 4 double, 1 family room **Facilities** sitting-room, dining-room, bar, library **Credit cards** not accepted **Children** accepted **Disabled** not advisable **Pets** accepted **Closed** never **Proprietor** Richard Loder

Tarragona

Masía del Cadet

This 15thC *masía* or manor house, has been restored by the Corominas-Vidal family with great care and intelligence and opened in 1990 as a model Catalan country hotel. Their act is unbeatable in the region, and at prices much lower than many other hotels in its class.

The family offers a friendly welcome, and the restaurant serves traditional Catalan cuisine.

An ideal base for a visit to Poblet's Cistercian monastery, a superb example of medieval architecture, which can claim to be a must for any visitor to this part of Spain.

Nearby Espluga museum; Poblet monastery (2 km).

Les Masies de Poblet, 43440, L'Espluga de Francolí, Tarragona
Tel (977) 870869
Fax (977) 870496
Location near Poblet monastery; car parking
Meals breakfast, lunch, dinner
Prices rooms PP; breakfast P; lunch PP, dinner PP
Rooms 12 double, all with bath; all rooms have central heating, telephone, radio, TV (optional)
Facilities dining-room, bar, TV room, sitting-room swimming-pool
Credit cards AE, DC, MC, V
Children welcome; play area in garden
Disabled access easy; lift
Pets not accepted
Closed never
Proprietor Mercè Vidal

Paradores in North-east Spain

The Pyrenees have a handful of remote modern Paradores. The most remote is the PT del Monte Perdido near Bielsa, hidden in a beautiful valley of bubbling mountain streams; the 24 rooms are appropriately rustic and the fireplace is the focal point (Tel (974) 501011). The PT Valle de Arán at Viella and the PT Don Gaspar de Portolá at Arties are separated only by 6 km of bumpy mountain road. Both come into their own in winter, serving the smart ski resort of Baqueira-Beret. The Viella Parador (135 rooms) has a semi-circular glass lounge to allow panoramic views (Tel (973)640100), and the Arties Parador (40 rooms) is stuffed with hunting trophies and easy chairs (Tel (973) 640801). Just south of Andorra is the PT Seo de Urgel; the modern hotel incorporates an ancient cloister, now filled with plants and functional sofas (Tel (973) 352000).

Further south are two impressive hilltop Paradores, at Cardona and Vich (see pages 70 and 76). And to the west, out of the mountains, the 66-room PT Fernando de Aragón in the captivating hilltop village of Sos del Rey Catolicó (the famous Fernando's birthplace) – one of the best modern Paradores (Tel (948) 888011). The modern 87-room PT de la Costa Brava at Aiguablava is chiefly remarkable for its splendid clifftop setting (Tel (972) 622162). Further south and a little way inland is the PT Castillo de la Zuda at Tortosa (tel.(977) 444450).

Tarragona

Country hotel, Espluga de Francoli

Hostal del Senglar

Built in 1965, this three-storey whitewashed and terracotta-roofed hostal is now almost completely obscured by the evergreen trees of its own garden, together with those of the neighbouring civic park.

It is a white-walled and wooden-beamed labyrinth inside. The many-chambered dining-hall, with its wooden balconies, nooks, crannies and murals of country scenes, is highly festive when full, and pleasantly intimate when not. The five-course *Menu de Calcotada* is an appropriately medieval feast - a traditional celebration of the vine and onion crops specific to the area (*calcots* is Catalan for shallots).

There is yet more timber and pottery in the salon, together with well-upholstered reproduction furniture from which the garden can comfortably be viewed. On Saturday evenings in August there is a splendid barbecue under the trees.

The bright bedrooms have stout wood and leather chairs, and decent-sized tables in addition to good, solid beds. Generous rugs add warmth to the red-tiled floors, and plants, pots and original oil-paintings are dotted around.

Nearby Poblet Monastery, (2 km); Museum of Rural Life in L'Espluga.

Pl Montserrat Canals, 143440, Espluga de Francoli, Tarragona
Tel & fax (977) 870121
Location up hill from main square in civic gardens; with garden and car parking
Meals breakfast, lunch, dinner
Prices rooms P-PP; breakfast P; lunch PP, dinner PP
Rooms 30 double, 10 single, 2 suites, all with bath; all rooms have central heating, phone, radio; some have TV
Facilities dining-room, sitting-room, TV room, disco; swimming-pool, tennis court
Credit cards AE, DC, MC, V
Children welcome; special menus; play area in garden
Disabled access easy; lift/elevator; ground-floor rooms **Pets** not accepted
Closed never
Manager Pedro Fernandez

Barcelona

Country house hotel, Cubelles

Llicorella

A modern building with steeply pitched slate roofs, surrounded by manicured lawns, the Llicorella oozes style and taste. As much as a hotel it is a gallery to display part of the owners' collection of contemporary sculptures and paintings.

The luxurious rooms are named after famous Catalan artists. Only two of them, the best as it happens, are in the main house. Room 16 is the *crème de la crème*, very large with French windows and an extensive terrace overlooking the front garden.

The rest of the rooms are in an annexe across the back lawn. Ask for room 12 which has two windows and a mirror which slides away to commuunciate with a sunken bath.

Most of the ground floor is taken up with the restaurant, which is rated amongst the top 200 in Spain. The three dining rooms traverse the house, opening onto the front lawn at one end and the swimming-pool at the other. House specialities include seafoods and homemade ice creams.

The sitting-room is more of a through passage between reception and the restaurant but you will be more than comfortable in your luxurious room.

Nearby Vilafranca del Penedès palace and wine museum (24km); Vilanova i la Galtrú (4km); Sitges (11km).

Calle San Antonio 101, 08880 Cubelles, Barcelona
Tel (93) 8950044
Fax (93) 8952417
Location on the outskirts of town; car parking and garden
Meals breakfast, lunch, dinner
Prices rooms PPP-PPPP; breakfast P; meals PPP
Rooms 15 double, all with bath; all rooms have TV, air-conditioning, minibar, central heating, safe, hairdrier
Facilities sitting-room, dining-room, swimming-pool
Credit cards AE DC MC V
Children accepted
Disabled access easy
Pets accepted (extra charge)
Closed restaurant only Sun dinner and Mon in winter
Proprietor Adriá family

Barcelona

Hotels in Barcelona

Most of the hotels in the lively and captivating city of Barcelona (which hosted the 1992 Olympic Games) are in the centre, in two areas – around the Plaça Catalunya and Las Ramblas (the broad, leafy avenue that leads to the sea), and around the cathedral and the medieval quarter (Barrio Gótico).

The Plaça de Catalunya has the more traditional grand hotels, such as the Ritz (Tel (93) 318 5200), an imposing building of 1919 with an abundance of gold-leaf and marble, and recently refurbished palatial rooms making it one of Barcelona's best. The Gran Vía (described on page 69) is another old charmer, as is the Avenida Palace (Tel (93) 301 9600), dignified and extremely popular, with excellent service and welcome. The Regente (Tel (93) 215 2570) has the added bonus of a roof-top swimming-pool. Further out, near the Francescá Macià Plaza, is a very British establishment, the Derby (Tel (93) 322 3215) which is smart and subdued, and, should you be in need, has Guinness on tap.

Of the Barrio Gótico hotels, the Colón (Tel (93) 301 1404) is an old favourite with tourists. It stands opposite the magnificent Gothic cathedral (ask for a front room with a balcony or a sixth-floor room with a terrace) and a stone's throw from many of the city's sights. Rooms have elegant high ceilings and comfortable furniture. The Suizo (described below) is not far from here.

Hotel Suizo

Just behind the cathedral, the Hotel Suizo could not be better placed. Inside it is really more *Parisien* than Swiss. Marble-topped tables, bentwood chairs and stools line the opulent wooden bar and fill the stylish cafeteria upstairs (where breakfast is served). The large restaurant is invariably busy; the four-course menu offers ample choice and changes daily. Attic bedrooms have the most character, with effective blinds on the skylights, and light parquet floors. Some of the other rooms have lino floors, but all are well furnished in dark oak. The staff can seem somewhat stretched, particularly at check-out time, but are helpful.

Nearby Cathedral, museums, Gothic quarter, Las Ramblas.

Plaza del Angel 12, 08002, Barcelona
Tel (93) 3106108
Location behind cathedral; car parking can be arranged
Meals breakfast, lunch, dinner
Prices rooms PP-PPP; breakfast P; meals PP
Rooms 44 double, 5 single, one suite, all with bath; all rooms have central heating, air-conditioning, phone, TV, minibar, radio, safe
Facilities dining-room, TV room, snack bar, sitting-room
Credit cards AE, DC, MC, V
Children welcome
Disabled access easy; lift/elevator
Pets accepted
Closed never
Manager Miguel Gargallo

Barcelona

City hotel, Barcelona

Hotel Gran Vía

In the hell of Barcelona's traffic, the Gran Vía could not be easier to find: entering the city from the airport, on the main street of the same name, you pass it on the right. A large town house, it does not look much from the outside, but once through the double-doored entrance, it is very grand. An impressive staircase sweeps up to the mezzanine, with its palatial dining-room in burgundy and grey and co-ordinating regency chairs. Here, English-speaking guests can have fun explaining to the Spanish-speaking matron who serves the extensive international breakfast how they want their bacon and eggs.

Above is another fine room – a salon with stucco ceiling and many antiques – and, true to Spanish form, there is a huge television stuck in the middle of the room. Beyond is a gorgeous roof terrace.

The bedrooms, set around the gallery, have all be renovated and refurbished recently. The air-conditioning is effective, if a bit noisy, and the Gran Vía displays the kind of ageing grandeur that is hard to resist. The staff remember you, and you remember them. The hotel is now under new management; we hope it does not change too much.

Nearby Las Ramblas; cathedral, museums.

Gran Vía 642, 08007, Barcelona
Tel (93) 318 1900
Fax (93) 318 9997
Location set back from Gran Vía, near Plaza Cataluña; with garden and car parking
Meals breakfast only
Prices rooms PP-PPP; breakfast P
Rooms 37 double, 11 single, all with bath; all rooms have central heating,
air-conditioning, phone, minibar
Facilities breakfast-room, sitting/TV room, terrace
Credit cards AE, DC, MC, V
Children accepted
Disabled no special facilities; lift/elevator
Pets not accepted
Closed never
Manager José Luis García

Barcelona

Hilltop Parador, Cardona

PT Duques de Cardona

Perched high on a hill above the Cardener river, this impressive medieval castle, built round an ancient collegiate church with parts dating back to the beginning of the 9th century, commands magnificent views in all directions, including the mountainous slag heaps from the potassium chlorate mine in the valley below.

The church itself is a popular tourist attraction, with guided tours morning and afternoon. But for local Spaniards, and some not so local, the main attraction is the food: an innovative menu and seasonal *carte* of house specialities and rare local dishes – country soups, rich fish stews, and desserts – served in the atmospheric stone-arched halls of the Bodegon restaurant (appropriately named, English-speaking visitors may think). Barcelonians will think nothing of driving the 100 km just to eat here.

There is little concession to medieval ascetism in other respects, though in terms of style, furnishings are faithful to the period of the building. Bedrooms range from extravagant suites with two four-posters to more modest twins, but all are immaculately furnished and clean. The three-chambered sitting-room is all rugs and leather armchairs, and free of TV. Staff put the comfort of their guests first.

Nearby Cardona; Salt Museum; Manresa (32 km).

Castillo s/n, 08261, Cardona, Barcelona
Tel (93) 869 1275
Tel (93) 869 1636
Location on hill top near Cardona, visible for miles; with garden and car parking
Meals breakfast, lunch, dinner
Prices rooms PP-PPPP; breakfast P, dinner PP
Rooms 52 double, 7 single, one suite, all with bath; all rooms have central heating, air-conditioning, phone, TV, minibar, safe
Facilities 2 dining-rooms, sitting-room, cafeteria, patio, 5 conference rooms
Credit cards AE, DC, MC, V
Children welcome
Disabled access difficult
Pets not accepted
Closed never
Manager Pedro Sonia

Barcelona

Hotel Sant Bernat

Hidden away up a tiny track off the winding Tona road, amid the dense low forest of the lush Montseny Sierra, this large, attractive terracotta-roofed villa, built in the 50s and now covered in vines, is a sleepy delight. The grounds are glorious, with a willow tree, pond and fountain to the front, and a stone terrace, and the charming little chapel of Sant Bernat behind. You can stand peacefully admiring the view, or listen to the water trickling down the mountainside.

Inside, it is equally serene, though at times the TV in reception is liable to intrude. A series of restful sitting-rooms with fireplaces, leather chairs and rugs lead past the bar to the comfortable dining-room, prettily decorated with floral upholstery, wooden panelled pillars and fresh flowers. The spotless bedrooms are equally attractive, and contain all the extras, from full-length mirrors down to a free comb.

Lunch and dinner involve a three-course fixed menu which changes every day, supplemented by a short but interesting *carte*. There are regular services in the chapel on Sundays and holidays, and special recitals on the feast day of St Bernard in June.

Nearby Montseny (8 km); Montseny Sierra.

Finca El Cot 08460, Montseny, Barcelona
Tel & fax (93) 847 3011
Location in mountains, up tiny road from Montseny to Tona; with garden and car parking
Meals breakfast, lunch, dinner
Prices rooms PP-PPP; breakfast P, dinner PP
Rooms 18 double, 2 family rooms, all with bath; all rooms have central heating, phone, TV, hairdrier, safe
Facilities dining-room, 2 sitting-rooms, bar
Credit cards AE, DC, V
Children accepted
Disabled no special facilities
Pets not accepted
Closed never
Manager Juan Miguel Pérez

Barcelona

Resort hotel, Vilanova i la Geltrú

Hotel César

A four-storey white building with green striped awnings over the windows, the César has been built up by the same family over four generations and more than 100 years.

Although from the outside it seems like just another block-shaped resort hotel, inside this one has a touch of taste without pretension. Classical music plays downstairs and the bar houses a small library.

The rooms are decorated simply but with interest using a variety of carefully chosen modern fabrics. All of them look onto the patio below and from the higher floors you can see the sea. The choice is the Albéniz suite on the first floor in which a fine china tea service and packet of Earl Grey awaits you in a homely sitting-room with cane furniture and a pine desk.

Much of the hotel's trade is from business groups and the public rooms reflect this with two conference rooms squeezing the sitting-room into a minimal area in front of reception. In good weather, however, the patio will meet most needs.

The restaurant, La Fitorra, is adjacent to the hotel in an old fisherman's cottage with a pleasant patio of its own at the back.
Nearby Casa Papiol, castle and Balaguer Museum; Sitges (7km); Vilafranca del Penedès palace and wine museum (20km).

Isaac Peral 4-8, 08800 Vilanova i la Geltrú, Barcelona
Tel (93) 8151125
Location behind Ribes Roges beach; car parking on street
Meals breakfast, lunch, dinner
Prices rooms PP-PPPP; breakfast P, meals from P
Rooms 28 double, 2 suites, all with bath; all rooms have air-conditioning, central heating, TV, minibar, phone, safe
Facilities dining-room, bar, 2 conference rooms, sauna/solarium, hydromassage pool
Credit cards AE, DC, MC, V
Children accepted
Disabled lift
Pets accepted
Closed restaurant only Sun dinner, Mon and Jan
Proprietor Esther Nolla

Barcelona

Hotel Romàntic

Gonçal Sobrer i Barea is passionately in love with his careful restoration of three 19thC town villas, originally built by Catalan rum barons returning from Cuba. He has good cause. This is a real rarity, and, considering it merits, very modestly priced. With its airy halls, blue and white tiles, sculptures, marble bays and ceramics, it could easily be the setting for a novel by García Marquez – or perhaps Graham Greene. In the club-style bar (the bar itself being an original imported from Cuba) you half-expect to spot Our Man From Havana sipping a rum while ensconced in one of the creaking wicker chairs.

Even the old stone washing troughs are preserved (though no longer in use). All the bedrooms are individually furnished with genuine antiques from the period, with original paintings and ceramics. Señor Sobrer is proud that they contain not a single 'mod con' (save, of course, *en suite* bathrooms), and there are few comfortable sofas; but this is the nineteenth century, after all.

Sadly, only breakfast is served in the palmed, patio-garden these days: a shame, since it would be a most 'romantic' setting for a longer, leisurely meal.

Nearby Old Sitges, museums, main beach.

Sant Isidre 33, 08870, Sitges, Barcelona
Tel (93) 894 8375
Location in side-street in heart of old city; with large garden, no car parking
Meals breakfast
Prices PP-PPP; breakfast P
Rooms 34 double, 30 with shower, 4 with bath; 18 single, 3 with wash-basin, 15 with shower; all rooms have phone, fans

Facilities 3 sitting-rooms, bar
Credit cards AE, V
Children welcome
Disabled no special facilities
Pets accepted
Closed 1 Nov to 15 Mar
Proprietor Gonçal Sobrer i Barea

Barcelona

Seaside hotel, Sitges

La Santa María

So successful is La Santa María in the centre of smart Sitges, that since our last edition it has expanded to having two restaurants – one on the seafront and the other in an internal garden – and almost doubled the number of bedrooms. It is still refreshingly unpretentious and invariably packed, with all kinds of customers enjoying local seafood and wines. From inside the atmospheric restaurants, glimpses can be caught of the kitchens. Giant wooden fans in the ceiling waft in the smells. Señora Uti – amazingly fluent in English, Spanish, French and German – reserves special treatment for her hotel guests, and is generally to be found behind the bar.

The hotel itself is modern, behind an older five-storey moulded plaster frontage, the chief advantage being that inside it is clean and bright rather than notably well equipped. In the bedrooms you will find pleasant wooden furniture, firm beds, good views and plenty of space. Here there is no hint of the restaurant bustle. In addition, a small TV room with leather armchairs, dotted with antiques, ceramics and magazines, provides a quiet backwater, as does the small sun terrace, where you can be alone with the geraniums.

Nearby Main promenade and beach.

Passeig de la Ribera 52, 08870, Sitges, Barcelona
Tel (93) 894 0999
Fax (93) 894 7871
Location on seafront in centre of promenade; car parking
Meals breakfast, lunch, dinner
Prices rooms P-PP; buffet breakfast P; dinner PP, lunch PP
Rooms 63 double, 4 single, 3 family rooms, all with bath; all rooms have phone, minibar, safe, TV, air-conditioning, central heating
Facilities dining-room, sitting-room
Credit cards AE, DC, MC, V
Children accepted
Disabled lift/elevator
Pets small dogs accepted
Closed Dec to Jan
Proprietor Antonìo Arcas

Barcelona

Country guest-house, Tavérnoles

El Banús

The ever-smiling Banús family have farmed on this site since 1214, and have a stout family tree proudly displayed in their hall to prove it. The rambling soft-stone farmhouse is modern by comparison – construction started as late as the 15th century. Antonio Banús is still making improvements, with a little help from his son – gently converting an adjoining barn into a dining-room and adding a downstairs room and bathroom for disabled visitors. Meanwhile his wife prepares the solid four-course dinner with similarly traditional skill.

Meals are served in the pantry-cum-bar in front of an open fire (highly welcome in winter). The ample breakfasts are also taken here, with a choice of continental bread or *pan con tomate y salchichon*, a local speciality which Antonio insists is nothing like pizza. Rooms, on the second floor, are appropriately basic, with no *en suite* facilities (there are four shared bathrooms) and furnished with a suitably catholic collection of family heirlooms, some delightful. Two self-catering apartments are also available. There is no midday meal, but the Banúses are more than happy to provide a picnic for those planning expeditions into the neighbouring foothills. The garden has some deliciously cool corners.

Nearby Vich (8 km); way-marked path to local sights.

08519, Tavérnoles, Barcelona
Tel (93) 812 2091
Location in heart of open countryside near Vich PT; with garden and car parking
Meals breakfast, picnic lunches, dinner
Prices rooms P; breakfast P; dinner PP; discounts for children
Rooms 6 double, one single, one family room; shared bathrooms; all rooms have

central heating
Facilities dining-room, sitting-room, bar; small swimming-pool, table tennis
Credit cards AE, MC, V
Children welcome
Disabled one room on ground floor
Pets well behaved dogs accepted
Closed one week in Sep
Proprietor Antonio Banús

Barcelona

Modern Parador, Vich

PT de Vic

Isolated on a steep mountainside overlooking the expansive Sau reservoir, this Parador de Turismo is an imposing grey stone edifice. Completed in 1972 to mimic a Catalan farmhouse, it is quite wrong in scale, but it is nevertheless not without beauty. The conservatory-style entrance gives way to a vast galleried hall with murals, polished wooden pillars and a stained glass ceiling worthy of Chartres.

The sons and daughters from the *masías* dotted throughout the surrounding *sierra* have their wedding receptions here. Walkers and cyclists with sufficient energy come in search of a little luxury and a comfortable bed to rest their limbs. They are rarely disappointed. Rooms are furnished in classical Castilian or Catalan style. Those with larger bathrooms have the unusual luxury of double basins.

The dining-room is another large hall with mock-medieval chandeliers, marble pillars, and more murals. The three-course menu of international, Spanish and Catalan dishes is enhanced by the magnificent view, and as night falls the sounds of the wilderness outside add atmosphere to the occasion. The staff serve with appropriate hushed efficiency.

Nearby Vich (15 km); walks to nearby sights.

Paraje el Bach de Sau, 08500, Vich, Barcelona
Tel (93) 8122323
Fax (93) 8122368
Location 14 km E of Vich, clearly signed from Vich; with gardens and parking for 30 cars
Meals breakfast, lunch, dinner
Prices rooms PPP-PPPP; breakfast P; meals PP
Rooms 30 double, 4 single, 2 suites, all with bath; all rooms have central heating, air-conditioning, phone, TV, minibar, safe
Facilities 2 sitting-rooms, bar, dining-room; tennis, swimming-pool
Credit cards AE, DC, MC, V
Children welcome
Disabled access easy; lift
Pets accepted
Closed never
Manager Senor Puigdollers

Gerona

Hotels on the Costa Brava

The 'Spanish Riviera' has emerged over the past 30 years as the Costa del Sol's major competitor for Spain's holiday trade. But, unlike the Costa del Sol, it is a naturally rugged coastline of rocky coves, sandy beaches, pine-clad cliffs and little fishing villages. For high season, book well in advance.

Blanes, the 'official' starting point of the Costa Brava, has many inexpensive hotels, pensions and campsites along one of the Costa's longest beaches. One of the best family hotels is the Park Blanes (Tel (972) 330250) secluded in pines, with a swimming-pool, tennis court and children's playground. Further up the coast, Lloret de Mar boasts an even longer beach and a even greater concentration of hotels, restaurants and nightclubs. If you want some solitude, try the 80-room family-owned Santa Marta (Tel (972) 364904), down a winding driveway in an area of private villas and botanical gardens. It is renowned for its seafood, eaten on the terrace overlooking the beach. Tossa de Mar has several smart little hotels, including two which merit detailed descriptions (pages 77-78). The 74-room S'Agaró Hotel (Tel (972) 325200) is a good second best in S'Agaró after the luxurious La Gavina (page 86). North of the Palafrugell area (which has an abundance of places to stay) are many smaller resorts with some reasonable (but not notable) hotels. The Almadraba Park (Tel (972) 256550) is a rather drab 3-storey hotel, but is in a delightfully peaceful spot on the bay of Rosas.

Readers' reports

Reports from readers are of enormous help to us in keeping up to date with the hotels in the guide – and other hotels that should be in it. The most helpful reporters are invited to join our Travellers' Panel, and to stay in listed hotels at little or no cost. More information on p11.

Gerona

Seaside hotel, Tossa de Mar

Hotel Diana

After the castle, the Hotel Diana is architecturally one of the most important buildings in Tossa. A family town house built on the central Plaza d'Espana in the 1850s, and backing on to the main promenade, it became a hotel a hundred years later. Today, when it opens for the summer season, it attracts an international clientele of art-nouveau-lovers.

The entire building is a tribute to the period, with a Gaudi roof faced with characteristic broken turquoise tiles, stained glass windows, a sweeping marble staircase and original Gaudi fireplace. The central salon contains art-nouveau frescoes, which have recently been restored, and a bronze fountain in naked female form by the Catalan sculptor Mares; light streams in through the glass roof three storeys above. The bedrooms are set in the surrounding gallery. With their high arched ceilings, marble floors and grand wooden shutters, they have plenty to offer in terms of style. Breakfast is taken either on the sea-front terrace or in the inner courtyard.

In 1989, after a period on lease, the Diana was returned to its original owners, a local hotel-owning family, who are continuing to carry out extensive refurbishment.

Nearby Castle; promenade; central beach.

Plaza d'España 6, 17320, Tossa de Mar, Gerona
Tel (972) 341886
Fax (972) 341103
Location entrance on Plaza d'España, rear entrance on beach promenade; no private car parking
Meals breakfast
Prices rooms PP-PPP; breakfast P
Rooms 20 double, one single, all with bath; all rooms have TV, phone, minibar; some with sea views
Facilities sitting-room, TV room,bar
Credit cards AE, MC, V
Children welcome
Disabled access easy; lift/elevator
Pets accepted
Closed Oct to May
Manager Fernando Osorio

Gerona

Town hotel, Bagur

Hotel Plaja

The Pujol family have made this appealing *auberge*-like hotel in the heart of old Bagur a modest treat. The two-storey building itself is over 80 years old and blends into its surroundings in typical Catalan style. Its pretty terrace with cork trees, roses and tubs of flowers is the main feature of the tiny plaza on to which it looks.

The restaurant inside oozes character, with its sandstone tiles, exposed beams and ceramics displayed in niches set into the walls. There is also a bar in here. Round the corner is a snug little salon with a fireplace, bench seats and more ceramics. Bedrooms are similarly cosy, but good use is made of the limited space, with reproduction pine furniture mixing well with the original pine shutters. There are the attractive, original green-and-white tiles in some of the rooms. Not all have *en suite* facilities though.

The restaurant is popular with residents and non-residents alike. The menu is a four-course affair supplemented by a comprehensive *carte* and local specialities on demand. Zarzuela (Catalonia's answer to bouillabaisse) is a particular favourite. Appetising smells waft from the kitchen at most times of the day. After breakfast a veritable task force of cleaners descend.

Nearby Castle; church; beaches (4 - 5 km).

Pl Pella i Forgas, 17255,
Bagur, Gerona
Tel (972) 622197
Location on tiny plaza in heart of old town; with parking for 10 cars
Meals breakfast, lunch, dinner
Prices rooms P-PP; breakfast P; meals PP
Rooms 8 double with bath; 8 single, 5 with bath
Facilities TV room
Credit cards MC, V

Children tolerated
Disabled no special facilities
Pets small ones accepted
Closed Christmas
Proprietor Narçis Pujol

Gerona

Town hotel, Bagur

Hotel Begur

Neat signs lead from 2 km out of Bagur to this 1960s conversion of a three-storey town house near the centre of the old quarter. Is it a tourist trap, or just a hotel that is unusually well organised? Fortunately, the cheery reception, personal escort to your room, fragrant towels and spotless sheets are quick to convince you that the Hotel Begur is very much the latter.

When we inspected, the immediate surroundings were marred by the construction of an underground car park, but inside, this fine old building retains many original features – central marble stairwell, arched stained glass window, tiled floors – and the character is maintained throughout. Some of the electrics are perhaps a little too antique, and at times the hot water can take a while to make its way through the old pipes, but in general the bedrooms are comfortable and of reasonable size.

The dining-room is smart and cool – netted curtains keep out the sun without obscuring the view. In summer, the substantial Catalan-Spanish three-course menu always starts with a hefty buffet salad. In winter there are soups. If you can find room for a fourth course, a choice can be found on the *carte*. All can be worked off with an evening stroll up to the castle.

Nearby Castle; church; beaches (4-5) km.

Comas y Ros 8, 17255, Bagur, Gerona
Tel (972) 622207
Location on hill by church and below castle, in heart of town; with parking for 6 cars
Meals breakfast, lunch, dinner
Prices rooms PP-PPP; breakfast P; menus PP
Rooms 30 double, 2 single, 2 family rooms, 2 suites, all with bath; all rooms have central heating, phone, TV

Facilities dining-room, 2 sitting-rooms, bar
Credit cards AE, DC, MC, V
Children welcome
Disabled lift/elevator; 3 ground-floor rooms
Pets small ones accepted
Closed never
Manager Rodolfo Castañer

Gerona

Seaside hotel, Aigua Blava

Hotel Aigua Blava

Too big to include in the guide but too distinctive to leave out, the Aigua Blava is a holiday village with a difference – a collection of delightful annexes among shady, pine-covered cliffs and flowered terraces, set round a tiny fishing harbour and beach, the whole arrangement is the opus of multi-lingual ex-swimming champion, Xiquet Sabater – a man whose life history would defy belief if it were not confirmed in the Spanish *Who's Who?*

The complex provides everything you need, even a boutique complete with genuine French assistance. Each room has individual style, ranging from summerhouse brightness in some annexes to the more formal bedrooms in the main hotel. Even the least inspiring are immaculate, and the sea views are out of this world. Guests who reserve a table in the pleasant terrace restaurant are rewarded with a feast of a four-course meal, with plenty of choice and desserts ranging from the holy to the sinful.

This area has always been Xiquet's home, and he wants his guests to feel the same warmth as if it were theirs, too. If the four generations who come back to this Mediterranean idyll year after year (making early booking essential) are any guide, he succeeds – with abundant help from his cheerful staff.

Nearby Bagur (5 km); beach.

Playa de Fornells, 17255, Aigua Blava, Gerona
Tel (972) 622058
Tel (972) 622112
Location in quiet spot near beach; with gardens and car parking
Meals breakfast, lunch, dinner
Prices rooms PP-PPPP; breakfast P; meals PP
Rooms 64 double, 8 single, 14 suites, 2 family rooms, all with bath; all rooms have central heating, phone; most rooms have air-conditioning
Facilities 4 dining-rooms, 4 sitting-rooms, 2 bars; swimming-pool, tennis courts, volley ball
Credit cards AE, DC, MC, V
Children welcome; play area
Disabled no special facilities
Pets small dogs accepted
Closed Nov to end Feb
Manager Juan Gispert

Gerona

Country inn, Castellç de Ampurias

Hotel Allioli

The setting for this country inn, in a dusty basin below the main Roses-Figueras road, could be better. But it could also be much worse: the neighbouring blue and white-washed Danone plant is almost picturesque as factories go. And the building itself more than makes up for its surroundings: a two-hundred-year-old Catalan farmhouse of considerable character.

Inside, the Peig Callol family have sympathetically fitted it out with antiques, lamps and benches, spiced up with fresh and dried flowers. Huge, whole dried Jamon Jabugos hams hang over the intimate bar to dry. The bedrooms display pure rural simplicity with linen counterpanes, exposed beams and whitewashed walls. But there are creature comforts too: clean *en suite* bathrooms, plenty of gadgets, and well-placed electric lights. The beamed four-chambered restaurant is well suited to the vast feasts local Spanish families come to devour on a Sunday. During the week Maria Callol will serve you a quieter, but no less sumptious Catalan meal, or even paella. Breakfast on the patio can be a very pleasant experience, provided the seasonal winds don't blow away your croissant. On such occasions, the bar is a safer alternative. Recent visitors to Allioli wrote that they were 'charmed'.
Nearby Figueras (10 km); Rosas (8 km).

Urbanización Castellonou
17486, Castelló de Ampurias, Gerona
Tel (972) 250320
Fax (972) 250300
Location in grounds set back from main Figueras/Roses road; with car parking
Meals breakfast, lunch, dinner
Prices rooms P-PPP; breakfast P; dinner PP
Rooms 31 double, 8 single, all with bath; all rooms have
central heating, air-conditioning, phone, TV
Facilities 2 dining-rooms, 2 sitting-rooms, bar
Credit cards MC, V
Children accepted
Disabled lift/elevator
Pets accepted in rooms
Closed 23 Dec to 10 Feb
Proprietor José Peig Rions and Maria Callol

Gerona

Town guest-house, Gerona

Hostal Bellmirall

Anna Pascual and Isidre Vicens run this diminutive guest-house, hidden away just to the right of the cathedral steps, as a family home, which it is. The house is a 14thC historic monument of ancient stone, which Anna and Isidre started converting to take guests in the 60s; they continue to make minor adjustments to this day. Isidre is supposedly the artist of the family, and his paintings, and those of Catalan colleagues, line the walls, and are displayed in a small gallery; his studio is on the top floor. But Anna's artistry is plain in the interior design which is all highly individual (the brightly decorated breakfast room and hand-made bedspreads are a joy), and in the breakfasts, which are also something special.

Anna and Isidre serve no other meals, though they offer the occasional beer, and advise (at length) on where to eat in the town. Service is highly personal, but this is not a hotel. Rooms have few *en suite* facilities and visitors who demand to see them before checking in risk being turned away. Anna and Isidre are busy enough with their satisfied regulars, and do not advertise. Indeed, it took an hour of pleading over a beer to elicit the information we needed for an entry here.

Nearby Cathedral; museums; old Gerona.

Calle Bellmirall 3, 17000, Gerona
Tel (972) 204009
Location in tiny street next to cathedral; no private parking
Meals breakfast
Prices P-PPP, breakfast P
Rooms 3 double, 2 with shower; 2 single, one with shower; 2 family rooms, both with shower
Facilities sitting-room, breakfast room

Credit cards not accepted
Children welcome
Disabled no special facilities
Pets not accepted
Closed 10 Nov to 6 Dec and 7 Jan to 5 Mar
Proprietor Anna Pascual and Isidre Vicens

Gerona

Seaside hotel, Palafrugell

Hotel Llevant

This unassuming three-storey house, right on the main promenade of the surprisingly unspoilt fishing village of Llafranc, was a restaurant before the Spanish Civil War. It had only six rooms when Jaume Farrarons took it over. Since then the family have built it up, and now they feel enough is enough, though they are planning a few minor improvements. Food is their true love, and heaven forbid that the hotel should start to overshadow the restaurant.

For the time being, at least, they have no need to worry: the Llevant's individual French-influenced Catalan cuisine draws a discerning crowd at all times of year. The excellent fish dishes are much enhanced by the sea air and sophisticated French café-style surroundings. The four-course menu will leave you staggering for a comfortable chair, which you will find without difficulty on the covered terrace adjoining, or in the small salon where exhibitions of local art are regularly housed.

If you are not up to the similarly proportioned buffet breakfasts of cheese and charcuterie, then a Continental breakfast can be taken in the bedrooms, which are simple but airy and tasteful.

Nearby Palafrugell (4 km); coastal walks; beach and harbour.

Francesc de Blanes 5, 17200, Llafranc, Palafrugell, Gerona
Tel (972) 300366
Location on main promenade in heart of village; no private car parking
Meals breakfast, lunch, dinner
Prices rooms PP-PPPP; breakfast P; meals PP
Rooms 22 double, 18 with bath, 4 with shower, 6 single, 2 with wash-basin, 2 with shower, 2 with bath; all rooms have central heating, TV; 18 rooms have air-conditioning
Facilities dining-room, sitting-room, bar, terrace
Credit cards MC, V
Children welcome
Disabled access difficult
Pets accepted in rooms
Closed Nov to 15 Dec; restaurant only, Sun night Jan to Mar
Proprietor Jaume Farrarons

Gerona

Hotel Sant Roc

High on the cliffs of Calella de Palafrugell, with magnificent views from the leafy terrace over the bay and steps down to the shore, the Sant Roc started life as a family home in the 1950s but was soon converted to an hotel, and has been expanded since. It is an appealing building, in style somewhere between a grand Catalan country house and a mini-monastery, featuring a terracota roofed tower.

It aims to be a family-run hotel run for families; guests are treated like old friends, and some return to the Sant Roc year after year. The interior is stylish, but pleasantly lived in. The wicker rocking chairs and antiques are there to be used, as is the more utilitarian furniture. You might find the wallpaper peeling in those rooms that are next on the list for re-furbishment, and not all of them have sea views, but they are clean, with original oil paintings on the walls and traditional Catalan wooden furniture painted in red, green or blue, known as polycromodo.

The three-course dinner and lunch menu has three choices for starter and main-course, and there is always the *carte* in the new panoramic restaurant.

Nearby Calella (0.3 km); Palafrugell (4 km); beach.

Pl del Atlántico, 2, Calella de Palafrugell, 17210, Palafrugell, Gerona
Tel (972) 614250/615286
Fax (972) 6140 68
Location on cliffs, set back from road amid trees; with garden and car parking
Meals breakfast, lunch, dinner
Prices rooms PP-PPP; breakfast P, dinner PP
Rooms 43 double, 2 single, 5 suites, 2 family rooms, all with bath; all have central heating, phone, TV, safe
Facilities dining-room, sitting-room, bar, terrace; table tennis
Credit cards AE, DC, MC, V
Children welcome; baby-sitting available
Disabled lift/elevator; ground-floor rooms
Pets accepted in rooms
Closed 15 Oct to 1 Apr
Manager Teresa Boix

Gerona

Seaside hotel, S'Agaró

Hostal de la Gavina

Set in secluded grounds on the edge of S'Agaró, above a small beach (with brightly painted huts, straight out of a 1930s musical, where the rich and famous rub sun-burnt shoulders with the merely affluent), this majestic Catalan villa is reminiscent of the great palaces of Europe, except that it is better cared for. A full description of the furnishings would read like a Christie's catalogue; as you wander through the circular formation of marbled salons and halls, the eye is met by enticing clusters of antique furniture, making it impossible to decide whether to continue or sit down. The immaculate bedrooms are all individually furnished in the style of your choice – Regency, rich walnut, Catalan polycromodo.

Not all is elegance. The 'El Barco' bar is, as its name suggests, built like the inside of a wooden boat. There are two restaurants, both serving the same Catalan/modern Spanish *carte* – one in French brasserie style, the other candle-lit, in plush Regency style – jacket and tie required.

Run by the son of the man who built it, the place is surprisingly relaxed for somewhere so opulent. The only thing to deter most people is the price.

Nearby Sant Feliu de Guíxols (4 km); beach.

Plaza de la Rosaleda, 17248, S'Agaró, Gerona
Tel (972) 321100
Fax (972) 321573
Location above beach on edge of main S'Agaró development; with gardens, and garaging for 14 cars and car parking
Meals breakfast, lunch, dinner
Prices rooms PPPP; breakfast PP; meals PPP
Rooms 55 double, 2 single, 16 suites, all with bath; all rooms have phone, TV, radio, minibar, hairdrier
Facilities 2 dining-rooms, sitting-rooms, bar, gymnasium, sauna, jacuzzi, terrace; sea-water pool, tennis courts
Credit cards AE, DC, MC, V
Children accepted
Disabled access easy; ground-floor rooms; lift/elevator
Pets accepted in bedrooms
Closed Nov to Mar
Manager Gustavo Jean-Mairet

Gerona

Seaside hotel, Tamariú

Hotel Hostalillo

This modern hotel is lifted out of the Costa rut by attention to detail and its tranquil location. Staff are friendly, efficient and helpful, the atmosphere welcoming – the hotel feels much smaller than its rule-breaking number of rooms would at first suggest.

Even from the outside, the Hostalillo is more than usually appealing: the five storeys are set into the steep hillside and pitched terracotta roofs help to break up the lines of the concrete.

The white walls inside give a cool, airy feel. The large split-level dining-room is flexible enough not to seem bare, even in low season. Here the four-course menu (constantly varied, with plenty of choice) can be struggled through, overlooking the inviting sun terrace full of geraniums and simple, comfortable chairs. Below is the once-picturesque fishing village of Tamariú, where the boats on the beach still out-number the frying bodies except in July and August. Steps lead through the garden, down the cliffs to the beach.

Bedrooms have all you can expect from a sound, basic beach hotel, including a view of the bay or the mountains.

Nearby Palafrugell (4 km); coastal walks; beach.

Bellavista 22, 17212, Tamariú, Gerona
Tel (972) 610250
Location on cliffs above village, overlooking Tamariú; with garden and parking for 13 cars
Meals breakfast, dinner
Prices rooms PPP-PPPP; breakfast P; dinner PP
Rooms 59 double, 2 single, 3 family rooms, 6 suites, all with bath; all rooms have phone; most rooms have central heating
Facilities dining-room, sitting/TV room, bar
Credit cards AE, MC, V
Children accepted
Disabled access difficult
Pets accepted
Closed 20 Sep to 1 May
Manager José M Biarge

Gerona

Country hotel, Viladrau

Hostal de la Glòria

This cosy country lodge was built over 50 years ago in simple Catalan style. Set just above the pleasant mountain village of Viladrau, with a pretty, peaceful garden terrace in front and the Sierra rising behind, it is a favourite with ageing Spanish card-players, who fill the inter-connecting small salons and leatherette armchairs at weekends throughout the year.

The Formatje family have decked the place out with copper pots, brass lamps, paintings and some fine old Spanish chairs, and keep the whole spotlessly clean. They are proud of their hostal, always eager to please, and genuinely apologetic when their rooms are full.

Rooms are simple and old-fashioned, with modern bathrooms. The four-course lunch and dinner menus are different each day, and are highly recommended. They are served in an attractive arched dining-room with a pretty tiled floor, wooden beams, green lace curtains and white walls hand-painted with birds and decorated with plates.

Overall, the result is an unpretentious home from home, where relaxation comes naturally – aided by the knowledge that rooms and meals are notably cheap.

Nearby Gerona (60 km); Vich (25 km); Montseny Sierra.

Torreventosa 12, 08553, Viladrau, Gerona
Tel (93) 884 9034
Fax (93) 884 9465
Location above mountain village in Sierra de Montseny; with covered car park
Meals breakfast, lunch, dinner
Prices rooms P-PPP; breakfast P; meals PP
Rooms 20 double, 3 single, one suite, 2 family rooms, all with bath; all rooms have central heating, phone, TV
Facilities dining-room, sitting-room, bar, swimming-pool
Credit cards MC, V
Children accepted
Disabled no special facilities
Pets not accepted
Closed 22 Dec to 7 Jan
Proprietors Eudald Formatje

Gerona

Country hotel, Figueras

Mas Pau

This creeper-covered family-run hotel is a converted 17thC *masia* (a large, well-to-do farmhouse) standing by itself in wooded and farmed countryside near the village of Figueras (made famous by Salvador Dali). It has been run by Nuria Serrat and her family since the 70s and, wedding parties permitting, you can be certain of friendly personal service.

The public rooms are essentially rustic, but decorated in *modernista* style, the Spanish equivalent of *art nouveau*. They include an arched bar (with painted mirrors, vases of ferns, wicker chairs around tables made from old sewing machines), and three interconnecting dining-rooms. The largest of these, the banqueting room, has a beamed ceiling and stone walls covered in old photos of Figueras. The seven suites look out on to tranquil gardens and cypress trees. They are decorated entirely in pink and grey; grey carpets, pink marble bathrooms and – according to Señora Serrat – curtains and bedspreads that change with the seasons: warm pink in winter, cool grey in summer.

In the well established gardens is a modest but attractive pool, with a shaded terrace on hand.

Nearby Figueras – Dali museum; Gerona (40 km).

Avinyonet de Puigventós, 17742, Figueras, Gerona
Tel (972) 546154
Location in countryside, 4 km SW of village of Figueras; with garden and car parking
Meals breakfast, lunch, dinner
Prices rooms PPP-PPPP; breakfast P; meals from PP
Rooms 7 suites, all with bath; all rooms have central heating, phone, TV, air-conditioning, minibar
Facilities dining-room, sitting-room, bar, banquet/conference room, terrace; swimming-pool
Credit cards AE, DC, MC, V
Children welcome; playground
Disabled easy access; some ground-floor rooms
Pets dogs accepted
Closed 8 Jan to Easter; restaurant only, Sun in winter
Proprietor Nuria Serrat

Gerona

Country house hotel, Torrent

Hotel Mas de Torrent

The setting of this stunning conversion of a 1751 Catalan *masia* is truly superb: in lush grounds concealing extensive terraces, pelota, paddleball and tennis courts, and the inevitable swimming-pool, amid open countryside, with views over Pals to the castle at Bagur beyond.

Just when you have come to terms with the exterior, you are confronted by further splendour inside. The style of the original interior is faithfully reproduced, but with a layer of luxury applied with impeccable taste. A series of arched salons with bright sofas and a fireplace gives way to the bar and terraces. Upstairs there are further spacious salons, with huge sofas and antiques, around which the individually named and styled rooms are set. 'Las Hortensias' is all antiques and lace, for example, while 'Las Dacias' is pure Barcelona chic. The 20 rooms in the garden bungalows have private, hedged terraces and more of a summerhouse feel. All are faultless in terms of facilities.

The dining-room which adjoins the main building is an impressive reproduction, with the exposed roof beams and slates typical of the region. There is an extravagant four-course menu and seasonal *carte* of Catalan, Basque and French cuisine.

Nearby Pals (4 km); Costa Brava beaches (14 km).

Afores s/n, 17123, Torrent, Gerona
Tel (972) 303292
Fax (972) 303293
Location near tiny village; with garden, car parking
Meals breakfast, lunch, dinner
Prices rooms PPPP; breakfast PP, meals PPP
Rooms 32 double, all with bath; all rooms have central heating, air-conditioning, phone, TV, minibar, radio, hairdrier, safe
Facilities dining-room, 4 sitting-rooms, games room; swimming-pool, tennis court
Credit cards AE, DC, MC, V
Children accepted;
Disabled access easy; specially adapted room and other ground-floor rooms
Pets accepted (extra charge)
Closed never
Manager Gregorio Berengui

Gerona

Town hotel, Bolvir

Torre del Remei

With considerable effort and impeccable taste, José María Boix and his wife, Loles Vidal, turned the Boix in Martinet into one of the most renowned restaurant-cum-hotels in the Catalan Pyrenees, and one of the top ten restaurants in Spain. Now they are repeating their success with this sumptuous mansion a short way from Puigcerdá.

The house, a colonial caprice of the *belle époque*, was built in 1910 and has been equipped as a luxury hotel by some of the most imaginative designers in Catalonia. The marble is from Greece; the furniture from Italy; the carpets from Tibet. Outside there is a 20,000 square metre garden planted with firs, towering redwoods, a swimming-pool and a putting green.

The Boix have created an oasis of elegance: expensive details abound – Bang & Olufsen video and TV, the selection of Loewe perfumes served by a valet. You will not lack creature comforts: the bathroom floors are heated and the king-size baths have hydromassage.

As you would expect, the cooking is also imaginative and appetizing. But the core of the appeal is most appreciated is the personal service that José María and Loles offer their guests.

Nearby S Domingo church; walls, town hall of Puigcerdá (3 km).

Camí Reial s/n, 17463, Bolvir de Cerdanya, Gerona
Tel (972) 140182
Location in the outskirts of Puigcerdá; garden and car parking
Meals breakfast, lunch, dinner
Prices rooms PPPP; breakfast PP; meals PPP
Rooms 4 double, 7 suites all with bath; all rooms have hydromassage, central heating, telephone, video,

TV (satellite)
Facilities dining-room, video library, private meeting room; swimming-pool, putting green
Credit cards AE, DC, MC, V
Children welcome
Disabled no special facilities; lift/elevator
Pets accepted in bedrooms
Closed never
Proprietor José María Boix and Loles Vidal

Zamora

Castle Parador, Benavente

PT Rey Fernando II de León

One look at the extraordinary sitting-room and you will probably excuse whatever shortcomings this hotel has. This voluminous hall occupies most of the old castle keep, the Tower of the Snail (the only part of the original building which was not destroyed by the French in the last century), which stands on a prominent cliff a short way out of town. Deep corner alcoves penetrate the turrets to reach snug stone benches by sunny windows. Large old tapestries adorn the walls. Overhead is a magnificent Mudejar coffered ceiling which was taken from a church.

A worn stone staircase (straight out of *The Name of the Rose*) takes you to another striking chamber below – the second bar, open only in the evenings – which has 2-metre thick walls, an enormous circular iron chandelier and some extremely interesting old furnishings.

The rest of the hotel, however, is modern and characterless in comparison. The dining-room and smaller bar have brick arches and a wall of windows giving views of fertile agricultural plains (shame about the flour mill immediately below). Twenty of the rooms have balconies sharing the same view.

Nearby Zamora (65 km); León (69 km); Puebla de Sanabria (84 km).

Paseo Ramón y Cajal s/n, 49600, Benavente, Zamora
Tel (980) 630300
Fax (980) 638303
Location on hill overlooking town; with garden and car parking
Meals breakfast, lunch, dinner
Prices rooms PPP-PPPP; breakfast P; meals PP
Rooms 28 double, 2 single, all with bath; all rooms have central heating,

air-conditioning, phone, TV, minibar
Facilities dining-room, sitting-room, 2 bars, TV room
Credit cards AE, DC, MC, V
Children welcome
Disabled access easy; 9 ground-floor rooms
Pets not accepted
Closed never
Manager Concepción Lechuga

Zamora

La Hostería Real de Zamora

Opened in 1990, the hotel occupies a 16thC palace next to an old stone bridge over the Duero, beside the city walls. The building was once the home of the Spanish Inquisition. A former inhabitant was Francisco Pizarro, discoverer of Peru.

The Hostería offers a remarkable amount of comfort for the age of the building, making it a reasonable alternative to the nearby Parador. Of special note is its beautiful claustral patio. The restaurant, adjacent to the old city walls, specializes in regional food with a strong Basque bias.

Nearby Romanesque churches; Gothic altarpiece, Arcenillas (6 km); 7thC Visigothic church, near El Campillo (20 km).

Cuesta de Pizarro, 7, 49001, Zamora
Tel (980) 534545
Fax (980) 5353
Location beside the ring-road connecting the roads to Galicia, Salamanca and Portugal; garden and car parking outside
Meals breakfast, lunch, dinner
Prices rooms PP; breakfast P; meals PP

Rooms 13 double, 2 single, one family, all with bath; all rooms have telephone, safe, minibar, radio, TV (satellite)
Facilities restaurant, meeting rooms, cafeteria
Credit cards AE, DC, MC, V
Children welcome
Disabled access easy to rooms 101 and 102
Pets accepted **Closed** never
Manager Yolanda Fidalgo

Paradores in Western Spain

The provinces of Zamora and Salamanca (around the NE corner of Portugal) have several pleasant Paradores which are described in detail in this section. In addition, Salamanca's modern white Parador sits on a hill above the town, traditionally the site of one of Castille's biggest cattle fairs. The best we can say about the hotel is that every guest room has a superb view of the town at night. Rooms are adequate and have sliding doors leading to small 'galleries' furnished with cane chairs (Tel (923) 268700).

The further south you travel, the fewer and further between Paradores become. The harsh terrain of Extremadura has kept the developers out from Roman times onwards, and only recently (and with a lot of funding from the EC, drawn to your attention on huge billboards at regular intervals) has the area been opened up by an extensive network of new roads. The existing Paradores, now more accessible, are all in ancient buildings – converted monasteries (Trujillo, Guadalupe, Mérida), hilltop castles (Oropesa, Jarandilla, Zafra) and a 14thC town house at Cáceres. Most have detailed entries. But when we visited, two potentially splendid castles – the imposing 15thC PT Hernán Cortés in the middle of Zafra (Tel (924) 550200) and the PT Virrey de Toledo, perched above the little town of Oropesa (Tel (925) 430000) – were closed for extensive renovations.

Zamora

PT Condes de Alba y Aliste

Zamora may seem out of the way for most visitors, but here is a hotel worth the detour. Much less interfered with than other Paradors occupying historic buildings, this palace surrounds a photogenic Renaissance courtyard fringed with carved stone pillars. The sunny enclosed halls and balconies along the four sides of the courtyard are decorated with antiques and pot plants (there are even plants sprouting out of an antique chest).

Many of the furnishings are original, or at least apt; the tarnished-green dining-room chandeliers have stags fleeing from their hubs. And at the foot of the stairs a complete suit of armour for a knight and his horse is on display. Most of the bedrooms have an old-fashioned feel; that is, they don't feel anonymously modern, but the number of rooms has doubled since our last edition. Some of them have double-doored windows opening on to the swimming-pool, others have canopied double beds, while the six suites available are as large as apartments.

The swimming-pool is open to the public, making this Parador feel less privileged than most others, particularly at weekends, when the pool can be busy (and noisy).

Nearby Romanesque churches; Gothic altarpiece, Arcenillas (6 km); 7thC Visigothic church, near El Campillo (20 km).

Plaza Viriato 5, 49001, Zamora
Tel (980) 514497
Fax (980) 530063
Location in main square; with garden and car parking
Meals breakfast, lunch, dinner
Prices rooms PPP-PPPP; breakfast P; dinner PP
Rooms 52 doubles, 6 suites, all with bath; all rooms have central heating, phone, TV, minibar
Facilities dining-room, 2 sitting-rooms, bar, terrace; swimming-pool (public)
Credit cards AE, DC, MC, V
Children welcome
Disabled easy access; lift/elevator
Pets accepted
Closed never
Manager Pilar Pelegrin

Salamanca

Hotel Conde Rodrigo

The Conde Rodrigo occupies a handsome 16thC stone-built palace on a leafy, historic square. It has, unfortunately, been insensitively modernized inside, obviously with the best of intentions. The bedrooms, though adequate, lack character but they offer some surprise extras, such as shoe-brushes in the bathrooms. It is popular for family functions, when the sitting-room is converted into a rowdy banqueting hall. There is also a disco in the basement. The restaurant serves a varied and economical menu. A sister hotel, Conde Rodrigo II, just out of town, is unashamedly modern, with its own pool and tennis court.
Nearby Plaza Mayor (short walk); Portugal (30 km).

Plaza de San Salvador 9, 37500, Ciudad Rodrigo, Salamanca
Tel (923) 461404
Fax (923) 48108
Location in square in historic centre, signed from Salamanca road; with small car parking area
Meals breakfast, lunch, dinner
Prices rooms P-PP; breakfast P; menu P

Rooms 31 double with bath, 4 single with shower; all rooms have central heating, phone, TV, minibar, radio
Facilities sitting-room, dining-room, bar, terrace, disco
Credit cards AE, DC, MC, V
Children Welcome
Disabled access easy
Pets not accepted
Closed never
Manager Ceferino Santos

Las Batuecas

A popular weekend destination for Madrileños, Las Batuecas is an imposing stone building located on the edge of the quaint village of La Alberca, in the heart of the fascinating Sierra de Francia, with its chestnut-woods and picturesque terraces of cherry-trees. The hotel begins on the first floor with a wide, covered terrace. Behind is a garden with a lawn and rose-clad trellis, and the rest of the floor is an open-plan lounge-bar- dining-room. The bedrooms and bathrooms have recently been refurbished and the windows sealed against the cold. A useful base for walking, cycling or touring.
Nearby La Alberca; Las Batuecas scenic road (40 km trip).

Carretera Las Batuecas, 37624, La Alberca, Salamanca
Tel (923) 415188
Fax (923) 415055
Location in village; with garden and car parking
Meals breakfast, lunch, dinner
Prices rooms PP; breakfast P; meals P-PP
Rooms 22 double, 2 single, 3 family rooms, all with bath; all rooms have central heating,

phone, TV, minibar
Facilities sitting-room, dining-room, bar, terrace
Credit cards MC, V
Children welcome
Disabled access difficult
Pets accepted only in bedrooms
Closed Jan to Mar
Manager Augustina Puerto

Salamanca

Castle Parador, Ciudad Rodrigo

PT Enrique II

Don't be disappointed if what you thought was the hotel – a stout tower with battlements – turns out to be only a warehouse. The hotel itself is the low-lying, attractively ivy-clad building beneath it. This was the second Parador to be opened, and the first to occupy a historic building. Fortunately, the present manager has paid more personal attention to it than many of those running other castles in the state hotel chain, and is still continuing to make improvements.

The rooms are spread out along two wings – one ancient, one modern. The former are reached by an arched curving white corridor; the 'star' is Room 10, a suite in which the bedroom is circular with a domed roof. Four of the rooms abut the old city walls and have views over the hotel's formal gardens. The public areas are decorated with occasional antiques, some suits of armour and plenty of green pot plants. The dining-room and sitting-room are both attractive, with partially sloping ceilings and wide basket-handle stone arches.

For pure history and a great view, don't forget to climb the tower. It is reached through the castle's original gate (ask for the key from reception), now in a splendid, crumbling state.

Nearby Plaza Mayor; Portugal (30 km); La Alberca (50 km).

Plaza del Castillo 1, 37500, Ciudad Rodrigo, Salamanca
Tel (923) 460150
Fax (923) 460404
Location on a quiet open square near centre of town; with garden and car parking
Meals breakfast, lunch, dinner
Prices rooms PPP-PPPP; breakfast P; dinner PP
Rooms 26 double, 1 suite, all with bath; all rooms have central heating, phone, TV, minibar
Facilities dining-room, 2 sitting-rooms, bar, patio
Credit cards AE, DC, MC, V
Children welcome; 20% discount for children under 10
Disabled access difficult
Pets not accepted
Closed never
Manager Angel Aliste

Cáceres

PT Zurbarán

Named after the 17thC painter, this Parador started life as a hospice in the 14thC, housing pilgrims who had come to venerate the Black Virgin of Guadalupe. The road through the hills has probably not improved much since their day, but the spectacular views of mountains and valleys – and of Guadalupe – make up for the hairpin bends and pot-holes.

The Parador is a simple, whitewashed building, centred around an open cobbled courtyard full of orange trees, with dozens of peculiar domed chimney-pots on its red-tiled roofs. Low arched doorways in the cloisters lead to a sitting-room on one side and a wood-beamed bar on the other. The dining-room, on the third side of the quadrangle, looks out through French windows on to lovely gardens. In summer, tables are set on the terrace, so you can eat and drink overlooking a water-garden and tiled pavilion beyond.

The modern concrete annexe of twenty bedrooms overlooks the gardens and swimming-pool. Rooms here are more spacious than those in the old part and all have balconies. But they do lack character, and it is always the original rooms that sell out.

Nearby 14thC Franciscan monastery (Zurbarán's paintings), mountain passes and surrounding countryside.

Marqués de la Romana 12, 10140, Guadalupe, Cáceres
Tel (927) 367075
Fax (927) 367076
Location opposite Franciscan Monastery, in middle of town; with garden and garage
Meals breakfast, lunch, dinner
Prices rooms PP-PPP; breakfast P; meals PP
Rooms 40 double, all with bath; all rooms have central heating, phone, TV, minibar, radio; most rooms have air-conditioning
Facilities 2 dining-rooms, sitting-room, bar; swimming-pool, tennis court
Credit cards AE, DC, MC, V
Children welcome
Disabled ground-floor rooms; lift/elevator
Pets accepted but not in dining-room
Closed never
Manager José Manuel Piña

Cáceres

Converted monastery, Guadalupe

Hospedería del Real Monasterio

The Hospedería is part of a 16thC monastery, which dominates the Guadalupe skyline. It is still a working monastery; Franciscan brothers live in one half of the building, guests in the other.

The bedrooms are set around a magnificent stone-arcaded courtyard. Many of them are the original monks' cells – long narrow rooms with high ceilings and low stone doorways. They are all different; some very elaborate, some very basic. On one side there is an exquisite suite full of ornate antiques, on the other, simple single rooms.

The public rooms downstairs are equally original; the sombre sitting-room contrasts with a cheerful white dining-room, with fresh flowers on every table. There is also a TV room arranged like a cinema, and an inviting bar with an arched roof and marble floor. Tables are set out in the courtyard among terracotta pots of geraniums and entwined giant cacti.

Although we arrived in the middle of a wedding reception for two hundred guests, the staff were not remotely put out and could not have been more helpful – the monks even gave us a guided tour of the monastery.

Nearby 14thC Franciscan monastery (Zurbarán's paintings); mountain passes and surrounding countryside.

Plaza Juan Carlos 1, 10140, Guadalupe, Cáceres
Tel (927) 367000
Fax (927) 367177
Location within monastery, entrance up a flight of steps from main road; parking for 30 cars
Meals breakfast, lunch, dinner
Prices rooms P-PP; breakfast P; meals PP
Rooms 40 double, one single, 5 family rooms, one suite, all with bath; all rooms have central heating, phone; some rooms have air-conditioning
Facilities dining-room, sitting-room, TV room, bar
Credit cards MC, V
Children welcome
Disabled ground-floor rooms, lift/elevator
Pets not accepted
Closed Jan 15 to Feb 15
Manager Fray Juan Luis Barrera

Cáceres

Converted castle, Jarandilla de la Vera

PT Carlos V

An imposing 15thC castle on the edge of a little white town
makes a perfect setting for a Parador – which is why the Carlos V
is often fully booked. The Parador architects have modernized it
without losing any of its medieval flavour; it is difficult to tell that
the new extension is not part of the original building. An arched
doorway between round towers leads into a cobbled courtyard.
Small shuttered windows peep out of cold grey walls and an
arcaded balcony looks down from solid square towers.

Most of the public rooms are simply furnished in a modern
style. Sombre oil paintings hang on the walls of the upstairs sitting-room, which opens on to the balcony set with yellow and
white chairs. The bar and dining-room are bright and comfortable, and look on to the Parador gardens. The original bedrooms lead off tall, narrow, beamed corridors and have all the
usual facilities. Rooms in the extension are light and spacious.

There is plenty to do outside; for the energetic, a swimming-
pool and tennis court; for children, a play area with swings and
slides; and for those who just want to relax, lovely rose gardens
surrounding this historic castle.

Nearby Yuste monastery (10 km); Trujillo, Cáceres, Avila, within
driving distance.

Avda García, Prieto 1,
10450, Jarandilla de la Vera,
Cáceres
Tel (927) 560117
Location at top of town, on a
rock with gardens around it;
with car parking
Meals breakfast, lunch, dinner
Prices rooms PPP; breakfast
P; dinner PP
Rooms 43 double, 10 single,
all with bath; all rooms have
central heating,

air-conditioning, phone,
TV, minibar
Facilities 2 dining-rooms, 3
sitting-rooms, bar; swimming-
pool, tennis court
Credit cards AE, DC, MC, V
Children welcome
Disabled ground-floor rooms
Pets not accepted
Closed never
Manager Miguel Fages

Cáceres

Town house, Trujillo

Mesón La Cadena

A smaller, cheaper alternative to the Trujillo Parador is the
Mesón La Cadena, on the main square. Situated in a rambling
16thC palace, it is really a restaurant (and noisy bar) with
rooms, rather than a hotel, but it merits inclusion because of
its central location and views over the square – a great place
for watching the world go by from tables set out on the cobbled
street.

The bedrooms are all on the third floor of this attractive
granite house, far enough away from the noisy bar to be assured
of a good night's sleep. They are simple and charming, with
dark wooden furniture and brightly coloured rugs, woven
locally. Rooms at the back have sloping ceilings, and look out
on to the hill leading up to the castle.

One floor below is the restaurant, on three sides of a tiny
internal courtyard, decorated with wrought iron lamps and
local pottery plates on white walls. It is a lively place in the
evenings, offering an interesting daily menu at a very reasonable price. The food is simple and good, and the waiters
are friendly. The bar on the ground floor is also a popular spot
and a good place to meet the locals.

Nearby Castle, palaces of the Conquistadors, old city walls.

Plaza Mayor 5, 10200,
Trujillo, Cáceres
Tel (927) 321463
Fax (927) 323116
Location on main square
in middle of town; car
parking in square
Meals lunch, dinner
Prices rooms PP; meals P-PP
Rooms 8 double, all with
bath; all rooms have central
heating, air-conditioning, TV
Facilities dining-room

sitting-room, bar
Credit cards AE, MC, V
Children welcome
Disabled access difficult
Pets not accepted
Closed never
Manager Juan Vicente
Mariscal

Cáceres

PT de Trujillo

Built in 1984 in the 16thC convent of Santa Clara, this is one of the newest and one of the loveliest of Spain's Paradores. The setting is perfect – it is away from Trujillo's busy main square, in a maze of quiet, narrow streets overlooking the plains of Extremadura, yet within easy walking distance of all the palaces and churches.

Some of the rooms are set in the old part of the convent, around a pretty courtyard full of orange and lemon trees. The cloisters lead off to a magnificent arched refectory through an ancient wooden door. This is now used as a bar and sitting area – a somewhat austere setting for writing postcards. The public rooms have been decorated with the convent in mind – furniture is simple, paintings are religious, and wooden crosses hang over the arches in the cloisters.

Half the bedrooms are in the nuns' old quarters, reached through low arched doorways from the gallery around the courtyard. The rest are in an adjoining modern building around a second courtyard which encloses an inviting hexagonal swimming-pool. Book early – this Parador is extremely popular.

Nearby castle, palaces of the Conquistadors, churches, old city walls and gates; Cáceres (50 km); Guadalupe (80 km).

Plaza de Santa Clara, 10200, Trujillo, Cáceres
Tel (927) 321350
Location on hill in narrow streets just outside town centre; with car parking and garage
Meals breakfast, lunch, dinner
Prices rooms PPP-PPPP; breakfast P; dinner PP
Rooms 45 double, one family room, all with bath; all rooms have central heating, air-conditioning, phone, TV, minibar, hairdrier
Facilities 2 dining-rooms, 2 sitting-rooms with TV
Credit cards AE, DC, MC, V
Children accepted
Disabled ground-floor rooms
Pets not accepted
Closed never
Manager Secundino Fuertes Alvarez

Badajoz

Town mansion hotel, Mérida

Hotel Emperatriz

Mérida is a lively historic town, although now (thanks to Moorish plundering of its stone) no more than half the size that it was in Roman times. The Emperatriz stands at its heart – a 16thC mansion, built of sandy-coloured granite in a privileged position on the main square.

The rather unprepossessing entrance opens into a grand cloistered courtyard, surrounded by granite pillars and arches on two floors. When we visited, dining-tables were laid in the courtyard for a wedding banquet – the effect was spectacular. The usual place to dine is an arched room off the cloisters, divided in two by elaborate wrought iron grilles. There are also two public bars, both underground, one serving *tapas*.

The hotel does not have all the facilities you expect in a Parador, but it has the character and sense of history that many of them lack. The bedrooms are all irregular shapes but are similarly furnished – embroidered bedspreads, wooden furniture and large bathrooms. Those with little balconies, facing on to the busy square full of outdoor cafés and ice-cream stalls, are rather noisy, at least by day.

Nearby Roman theatre, arena and villa, Alcazaba; Badajoz (60 km), Zafra (65 km), Cáceres (70 km), Trujillo (90 km).

Plaza de España 19, 06800, Mérida, Badajoz
Tel (924) 313111
Fax (924) 313305
Location on main square (follow signs to town centre); no private car parking
Meals breakfast, lunch, dinner
Prices rooms PP; breakfast P; meals PP
Rooms 17 double, 24 single, one family room, all with bath; all rooms have central heating, phone
Facilities dining-room, TV room, 2 bars
Credit cards V
Children welcome
Disabled no special facilities
Pets welcome
Closed never
Manager Francisco Moro

Badajoz

PT Vía de la Plata

Mérida's chequered history is reflected in almost every room of the Parador Vía de la Plata (named after the Roman road it was built on). Roman friezes, acanthus capitals and ceramic urns come from the Augustan temple and Praetorian palace that stood here in Roman times. Visigothic stones and columns are evidence of a governor's residence, while Arabic inscriptions and decorations reveal later Moorish occupation. In the 16th century the Military Order of Santiago rebuilt the ruins as a monastery and their chapel now makes a stunning lounge. Although much of the Parador is modern, it is difficult not to get caught up in its intriguing web of history.

It stands on a quiet shady square, a short walk from the heart of town. Reception opens on to a pretty, typically Andalucian courtyard and a passage-way leads through to Moorish gardens. Most bedrooms look over the gardens, and are pleasant and spacious, with large marble bathrooms. Endless corridors lead to public rooms – a high-ceilinged sitting-room contrasting with a low beamed bar. All were busy when our inspectors visited, especially the dining-room, serving mouth-watering meals.

Nearby Roman theatre, arena and villa, Alcazaba; Badajoz (60 km), Zafra (65 km), Cáceres (70 km), Trujillo (90 km).

Plaza de la Constitución 3, 06800, Mérida, Badajoz
Tel (924) 313800
Location on quiet grassy square, in middle of old town; with garden and car parking
Meals breakfast, lunch, dinner
Prices rooms PPPP; breakfast P; meals PPP
Rooms 79 double, one single, 2 family rooms; all rooms have central heating, air-conditioning, phone, TV, minibar, radio
Facilities 3 dining-rooms, 5 sitting-rooms, 2 bars; swimming-pool, sauna, gymnasium
Credit cards AE, DC, MC, V
Children welcome
Disabled lift/elevator
Pets not accepted
Closed never
Manager Victor Teodosio

Badajoz

Town hotel, Zafra

Hotel Huerta Honda

When our inspectors visited Zafra, the castle Parador was surrounded by scaffolding and in the throes of extensive redecoration. So they were delighted to discover, right next door, the Huerta Honda. This white villa, with red-tiled roofs and windowboxes dripping with geraniums, has fine views of the medieval castle. It is not merely a decent substitute for the Parador; in many ways, it is more attractive.

The hotel is built around a swimming-pool – the bedrooms on three sides, the dining-room on the fourth. Chairs and tables spill out of the bar and sitting-room around the pool, and it is a perfect place to enjoy a drink, between potted plants and trailing ivy. If you have had too much sun, you will appreciate the cool sitting-room, full of wicker furniture and wonderful ornaments (look out for the wicker pig under the mini grand piano, and the boar's head over the open fire). The dining-room is a similar haven, and the *menu del dia* excellent value. The hotel bar is a popular night spot and positively buzzes with activity. In contrast the bedrooms are serene; decorated in pastel shades with every possible comfort. You can be sure of a good night's sleep and of waking to a great view.

Nearby Llerena (40 km), Aracena (90 km).

Av López Asme 30, 06300, Zafra, Badajoz
Tel (924) 554100
Tel (924) 552504
Location next to castle Parador in heart of town; with car parking
Meals breakfast, lunch, dinner
Prices rooms PP-PPP; breakfast P; meals PP
Rooms 37 double, 29 with bath, 8 with shower; 9 single with shower; one family room with bath; all have central heating, air- conditioning, phone, TV, minibar, radio, hairdrier **Facilities** dining-room, 2 sitting-rooms, 3 bars, terrace; swimming-pool
Credit cards AE, DC, MC, V
Children accepted
Disabled access easy; ground-floor rooms; lift/elevator
Pets accepted **Closed** never
Manager María Encaruación Esteban

Segovia

Las Sirenas

Built in the 1950s as Segovia's 'grand hotel', Las Sirenas has never quite made it to the top but fails gloriously in the attempt. (You will still find most of the interior glass doors ostentatiously etched 'GHLS' – Grand Hotel Las Sirenas.) The whole place is attractively faded and tarnished, and full of life, making Segovia's might-have-been far more appealing than many of the city's more modern and expensive lodgings, though a recent visitor found the atmosphere rather impersonal and unwelcoming.

You will probably spend most of your time padding down long corridors, finding out where everything is. The building, with its long, wide entrance hall dotted with armchairs, pot plants and the odd grandfather clock, and its ceremonial staircase with padded handrail, includes a smoke-filled gentleman's club (or 'casino'), a cinema and a barber's shop. The sitting-room has a pleasant terrace bordered by wooden banisters: a quiet corner for breakfast. The bedrooms, simple and functional – often with parquet floors, polished mahogany furniture, substantial beds and new bathrooms – recall scenes from 1950s films. They are comfortable but not luxurious, and have a poor choice of lighting. Most are double glazed to keep out both the cold and noise.

Nearby Alcázar and aqueduct; La Granja (10 km).

Juan Bravo 30, 40001, Segovia
Tel (921) 434011
Location on square of same name, in front of church of San Martin; with car parking
Meals breakfast
Prices rooms PP; breakfast P
Rooms 24 double, all with bath; 9 single, 6 with bath, 3 with shower; 3 suites, 3 family rooms, all with bath; all rooms have central heating, air-conditioning, phone

Facilities sitting-room, bar, games room, terrace
Credit cards AE, DC, MC, V
Children welcome
Disabled access easy; lift/elevator
Pets not accepted
Closed never
Manager Jesus Escudero

Segovia

Converted mill, Collado Hermoso

El Molino de Río Viejo

This old mill set amongst poplars by the River Viejo makes a perfect base from which to explore the leafy countryside of Segovia. Horses are available to riding enthusiasts.

The bedrooms, some with beamed attic ceilings, are all the more cosy for the absence of mini-bar and TV. The dining-room is in the old mill room. From Monday to Thursday only pre-requested cold meals are served, but at the weekends you can try the chef's roast lamb and home-made strawberry tart.

Booking is essential. At weekends the hotel is very popular. At other times it may be closed if there are no reservations.

Nearby Sotosalbos (1 km); Pedraza (12 km); Segovia (18 km).

Carretera N110, km 172, 40170, Collado Hermoso, Segovia
Tel (921) 403063
Fax (921) 403051
Location beside a main road; garden and car parking
Meals breakfast, lunch, dinner
Prices rooms PP; full board PPP; breakfast P
Rooms 6 double, 4 with bath, 2 with wash-basin, 2 single
with wash-basin; all rooms have central heating
Facilities sitting-room, bar, dining-room; satellite TV, library
Credit cards AE, V
Children welcome
Disabled access difficult
Pets accepted
Closed never
Proprietor Coloma Armero

Paradores in Central Spain

The three provinces to the north-west of Madrid have a handful of interesting Paradores. The 73-room one at Tordesillas is a low modern building set in a secluded pine-grove, just out of the town; it makes a good base for exploring this very interesting region of castles and medieval towns (Tel (983) 770051). Within easy reach of it is the PT de Segovia – modern, 80 rooms, on the edge of a lake, fine views of the town and cathedral (Tel (911) 430462). Near Avila is the 15thC PT Raimundo de Borgoña (see page 110) and, in the Sierra de Gredos, the rustic PT de Gredos near Navarredonda de Gredos, with its beamed ceilings and mounted hunting trophies (Tel (918) 348048).

With one exception, the Paradores to the north-east of Madrid (Soria and Sigüenza) and to the south (Chinchon, Toledo, Almagro, Alarcón) are all described in detail in this section. The exception is the unremarkable PT de Manzanares, east of Ciudad Real, which is a large white modern building in shady grounds (Tel (926) 613600).

Segovia

Village hotel, Pedraza de la Sierra

La Posada de Don Mariano

If it is a quiet night, the manager of this archetypal charming small hotel, may offer you a selection of rooms. The trouble is: which one do you choose if all of them are like showpieces from an antiquated Ideal Home Exhibition?

Each is unique, personal, luxuriously carpeted and decorated with English floral wallpaper. Antiques abound. Everything is carefully arranged and prepared so that you could almost forget you are in a hotel. It comes as no surprise to learn that the hotel was designed by the owner of one of Madrid's most famous furnishing shops and was featured in *Elle* magazine. But that does not help you choose your room. Maybe you should just take your chance. How about one of the attic rooms upstairs? Smaller perhaps, but still exquisitely furnished and oozing with character. TVs are only provided on request – otherwise they spoil the decoration.

We had three minor reservations about the hotel: the noise from the bar below seems to travel to the rooms above it; the bathrooms are inadequately lit; and breakfast is disappointing. Otherwise, this is a hotel to remember.

Nearby Castle and square (2 mins walk each); scenic road up to Puerto de Navafría in the Sierra de Guadarrama (30 km).

Calle Mayor 14, 40172, Pedraza de la Sierra, Segovia
Tel & fax (921) 509886
Location near castle in main street; no private car parking
Meals breakfast, lunch, dinner
Prices rooms PP-PPP; breakfast P; meals *à la carte*
Rooms 15 double, 3 single, all with bath; all rooms have central heating, phone, TV (on request)
Facilities dining-room, sitting-room/bar
Credit cards AE, DC, MC, V
Children welcome
Disabled access difficult
Pets not accepted
Closed never
Manager Mariano Pascual

Soria

Modern Parador, Soria

PT Antonio Machado

Prettily located, hanging off the side of a very green hilltop park, this modern brick-built Parador could be seen as a short guide to modern Spanish literature. It is named after the poet who lived and wrote in Soria but died in exile; you will find his blown-up image and his more famous poems on many of the pinkish walls.

Unlike most other modern Paradors, this one has not been contrived to look old. The furniture is as recent as the building and is occasionally brash and uncomfortable – but it may come as something of a relief after the rustic Castilian style of so many other Paradors. And if the hotel is short on charm, it has the compensating virtue of small size.

The entrance and reception are half-way up the building. There are bedrooms on the two floors above it and on one below. The higher up you go, of course, the better the view: 12 of the higher rooms offer vistas of Soria and the surrounding woodland; the rest are too low to see much from, or else look directly on to the quiet one-way road around the park outside. The dining-room and sitting-room are open-plan, separated by a wooden screen and sharing the same high, sloping ceiling; noise, unfortunately, travels easily between them.

Nearby: San Juan de Duero monastery (1.5 km).

Parque del Castillo s/n, 42005, Soria
Tel (975) 240800
Fax (975) 240803
Location on hill overlooking city and Duero river; with car parking
Meals breakfast, lunch, dinner
Prices rooms PP-PPPP; breakfast P; meals PP
Rooms 28 double, 4 single, 2 suites, all with bath; all rooms have central heating, phone, TV, minibar
Facilities dining-room, 2 sitting-rooms, bar
Credit cards AE, DC, MC, V
Children welcome
Disabled access impossible
Pets not accepted
Closed never
Manager Emilio Lafuente

Ávila

City hotel, Ávila

Gran Hotel Palacio Valderrábanos

From its grand 15thC stone doorway, surmounted by an aristocratic family crest, to a room with a private tower, this spacious
and calm hotel is pervaded by its past. Over reception you will
find a graceful stone arch and old painted beams. In the hall, a
glass case crammed full of antiques and curios for sale makes
souvenir hunting easy.

The older, cosier rooms have floral wallpaper and beech furniture, but they occasionally feel uncomfortably half-empty. The
thick shutters – which cut out noise – also shut out the daylight
(the modern rooms on the third floor are much lighter). Some
of the rooms have views across the square to the magnificent
door of Ávila cathedral. But the real treat among them is room
229, from which a staircase ascends to a secluded sitting-room in
the former watch-tower.

The slightly rustic white-walled restaurant in the basement
(more attractive than the marbled dining-room upstairs) could
be a museum of cookery – its intriguing exhibits including gigan-
tic wine pots, an old sausage press (medieval, we were assured)
and a vintage cheese churn.

Nearby Cathedral (opposite hotel), city walls (5 mins walk), St
Thomas' Monastery (short drive); Guisando stone bulls (70 km).

Plaza Catedral 9, 05001, Ávila
Tel (920) 211023
Fax (920) 251691
Location next to cathedral in
middle of town; no private car
parking
Meals breakfast, lunch, dinner
Prices rooms PPP-PPPP;
breakfast P; meals PP
Rooms 62 double, 8 single, 3
suites, all with bath; all rooms
have central heating,
air-conditioning, phone, TV,

minibar, radio, hairdrier
Facilities 2 dining-rooms,
3 sitting-rooms, bar
Credit cards AE, DC, MC, V
Children welcome
Disabled access easy;
lift/elevator
Pets accepted
Closed never
Manager Tomás Beltrán

Ávila

City Parador, Ávila

PT Raimundo de Borgoña

In a corner of the old town, nestling against the city walls, this Parador is a careful mixture of old and new. Only the distinctive tower, and the shady courtyard with its tall pine tree, are left of the original 16thC building.

The rooms, like the building, divide into the old and the new. Those in the tower are somewhat cramped, with squeaky wooden floors. Those in the modern wings are larger, lighter and have better views. Some have four-poster beds. In others, the bed-frames look as if they had been made from sawn-up portcullises. In spring, birdwatchers should ask for room 209, from which there is a good view of storks nesting on an old belltower between March and June.

There are not many inviting places to sit indoors, but there is a sunny terrace outside the bar, and the courtyard is always fresh and cool. From the hotel it is only a short stroll to Ávila's famous city walls.

The restaurant serves a special dessert: soft, sweet balls named after Ávila's famous daughter – 'Saint Teresa's Yolks'.

Nearby Polentinos Palace and cathedral (5 mins walk); St Thomas' Monastery (a short drive); Guisando stone bulls (70 km); Sierra de Gredos (80 km).

Marqués de Canales y Chozas 2, 05001, Ávila
Tel (920) 211340
Fax (920) 226166
Location near old walls in middle of city; small car park
Meals breakfast, lunch, dinner
Prices rooms PPP-PPPP; breakfast P; meals PP
Rooms 59 double, 3 single, all with bath; all rooms have central heating, phone, TV, minibar, hairdrier

Facilities dining-room, sitting-room, bar, patio
Credit cards AE, DC, MC, V
Children welcome
Disabled access difficult; lift/elevator to 5 rooms
Pets not accepted
Closed never
Manager Juan de la Torre Alcalá

Madrid

Hotels in Madrid

Hotels in the city of Madrid cannot be conveniently divided into districts; they spread throughout the central area. The heart of the city is bounded by the Palacio Real and the railway terminus of the Estación del Norte on the west, and the wonderful Prado museum and gardens of El Retiro on the east, with the plaza of the Puerta del Sol roughly in the middle.

The Arosa (Tel (91) 532 1600) is a stylish building on the Gran Via, close to the Puerta del Sol. The rooms are elaborately decorated and well soundproofed to minimise noise from the busy street below. Also close to the Puerta del Sol is the Reina Victoria (Tel (91) 531 4500), an old favourite, with 120 reasonably priced rooms. The best of these overlook the pretty little plaza of Santa Ana.

Madrid is not blessed with the little gem-like hotels that are such a feature of Paris, Venice or Florence, for example. Real quality tends to go hand in hand with size and grandeur (and expense). For a once-in-a-blue-moon treat, there is the Ritz (Tel (91) 521 2857), which has been beautifully restored to reflect its former early-19thC glory. Public rooms are decorated with priceless carpets and tapestries, bedrooms are filled with antiques, service is absolutely immaculate; this is one of Spain's top hotels, a fact reflected in its prices. Nearby is the equally grand but rather less wonderful Palace (Tel (91) 429 7551), a massive 500-room hotel with an impressive clientele – from matadors to politicians. Service tends to be (not surprisingly) rather impersonal, but like the Ritz it has an excellent location close to the Prado. In contrast, the Villa Magna (Tel (91) 561 4900) is further from the middle towards the northern district. It is a modern version of the Ritz, and almost as classy. Set in immaculate gardens, it has a glass and steel tower, public rooms decorated in 18thC style, large bedrooms and stylish dining-rooms.

Outside the central area, there are two hotels worth mentioning. The Monte Real (Tel (91) 216 2140) is a modern hotel in an exclusive suburb. Ask for one of the rooms that overlooks the pool surrounded by trees in tranquil gardens. The hotel is far more impressive from the inside than from the outside; walls are hung with fabulous works of art and tapestries. The Barajas (Tel (91) 747 7700) is 14 km from the middle of the city, near the airport – ideal for anyone with an early flight. It has excellent facilities, including a swimming-pool, gymnasium, golf course and gardens.

Paying by credit card
We say in our factboxes which credit cards are accepted. Whether you do or do not value the free credit gained when paying by card, there are other advantages, particularly when making a payment in advance. Provided the card is a genuine credit card which permits you to borrow money for an extended period (Visa, Mastercard) and not a charge card which lacks that facility (American Express, Diners Club), paying with the card makes the credit card company jointly liable for fulfilment of your contract with the hotel. If you are not given the kind of room you wanted, for example, you can pursue a claim against the credit company when you get home.

Madrid

City hotel, Madrid

Hotel Carlos V

At first sight this looks like a run-of-the-mill city-centre hotel and indeed the bedrooms, though spotless and well-equipped with bright modern bathrooms, are impersonal. Scratch the surface, however, and you will find a family-run hotel that cares for its individual guests. The original owner's grandson, now in charge, eschews organised tour groups.

The hotel has a great variety of bedrooms including ones that interconnect and family rooms. Some rooms on the first and second floors have small balconies and five rooms at the top of the building have fair-sized, sun-catching terraces for no extra charge. The Carlos V is also one of the few hotels in its class in Madrid to have plenty of double beds. The hotel's greatest asset is its stylish sitting-room with its crystal chandeliers, large mirrors and moulded ceiling.

In a pedestrianized street next to the Puerta del Sol ('the centre of Spain'), the Carlos V can be a maddening place to find in a car. The convenient location has its disadvantages. A good night's sleep in summer depends on getting the right balance between ventilation, street noise and the din of the air-conditioning.

Nearby Metro (Callao or Sol, 2 mins walk), Plaza Mayor.

Maestro Vitoria 5, 28013, Madrid
Tel (91) 531 4100
Fax (91) 531 3761
E-mail hotel.carlosv@tsai.es.
Location on a pedestrianized street near Puerta del Sol; public car parking nearby
Meals breakfast
Prices rooms PPPP; breakfast P
Rooms 61 double, 6 single, all with bath; all rooms have central heating, air-conditioning, phone, TV, radio
Facilities sitting-room, bar/breakfast room
Credit cards AE, DC, MC, V
Children welcome
Disabled access easy; lift/elevator
Pets not accepted
Closed never
Proprietor Nicolás Gutierrez

Madrid

City hotel, Madrid

Hotel Serrano

On a side street off Madrid's prestigious, modern north-south axis, the Paseo de la Castellana (the place to be seen these days), the Serrano is a small hotel for anyone in search of a little non-central exclusivity.

The building – unashamedly modern, with a grimy façade – is well designed inside, with plenty of light and space. Moreover, it has been conscientiously decorated and furnished, often with reproduction period chairs and tables. There are also a few genuinely antique objects. The large, sombre 18thC tapestry on the wall of the sitting-room-cum-bar is, we were assured, a priceless national treasure.

In a Spanish city hotel with so few rooms, you can expect some extras – such as special massage showers in all bathrooms. The three suites are moderately luxurious; their sitting-rooms alone are bigger than many entire hotel rooms. There are even magazines on the coffee tables – a personal touch for a chain hotel.

Warts and all, here you get the feeling that you are one of a very few select guests and can make yourself a little at home. A modest alternative to the Ritz at a fraction of the price.

Nearby Metro (Rubén Darío station, 5 mins walk); the Prado and Retiro Park (2 km); Plaza Mayor and old city centre (3 km).

Marqués de Villamejor 8, 28006, Madrid
Tel (91) 435 5200
Fax (91) 435 4849
Location in a quiet street near Paseo de la Castellana; no private car parking
Meals breakfast
Prices rooms PPP-PPPP; breakfast P
Rooms 24 double, 5 single, one family room, 4 suites, all with bath; all rooms have central heating, air-conditioning, phone, TV, minibar, hairdrier, safe
Facilities sitting-room/bar
Credit cards AE, DC, MC, V
Children welcome
Disabled access difficult; lift/elevator
Pets not accepted
Closed never
Manager Laura Gil

Madrid

Converted monastery, Chinchón

PT de Chinchón

Gathered around a light, green, airy courtyard – with tall cypress trees in its corners and pigeons flitting around a fountain and climbing roses – the ground floor of this 17thC monastery is a wealth of colour and detail. The peaceful, glazed-in cloisters form wide passages which are decorated with murals and antiques: clocks, chests, cabinets, even a large old brass still (the town is renowned for its *anis*).

The stately dining-room and cool blue bar are both brightly tiled and lit by small windows piercing massively thick walls. Climb the staircase, which has original but fading frescoes on the ceiling above it, and you find landings furnished with comfortable sofas.

The bedrooms are different in style from everything else. They have the austere but romantic atmosphere of a decaying medieval palace: very clean, but deliberately made to look as if they were a little dusty; with the shutters closed tightly, little daylight penetrates the gloom. The floors are covered with earth-red tiles and the blue wooden furniture is brightly painted with golden garlands – quite out of character with the nobility of the ground floor. They have generously-sized Parador bathrooms.

Nearby Plaza Mayor; Royal Palace, Aranjuez (26 km).

Avenida Generalisimo 1, 28370, Chinchón, Madrid
Tel (91) 894 0836
Fax (91) 894 0908
Location opposite main square in heart of village; private garage
Meals breakfast, lunch, dinner
Prices rooms PPPP; breakfast P; meals PP
Rooms 38 double, all with bath; all rooms have central heating, air-conditioning, phone, TV, minibar, hairdrier
Facilities 2 dining-rooms, sitting-room, bar, terrace
Credit cards AE ,DC ,MC, V
Children welcome
Disabled access not easy; some ground-floor rooms
Pets not accepted
Closed never
Manager José Menguiano

Madrid

Converted cloister, El Paular

Hotel Santa María del Paular

You don't often get the chance to stay in a four-star hotel next to – and sharing its premises with – a Benedictine monastery. The Santa María occupies the old cloisters, entered by means of a monumental arch.

Sadly, the chain that runs this hotel is more interested in its up-market facility-rich image than in artistic heritage. The mock-historical style of decoration scarcely does justice to the handsome surroundings. You will just have to use your imagination. But it is a peaceful place, surrounded by trees and with plenty of space to stretch out – a popular location for conferences and wedding receptions. There is also a choice of places to eat. Apart from the dining-room, a *méson* offers lamb cooked in the traditional way, in a wood-fired oven.

The bedrooms are simple, sober and Castilian in style –which in this part of the world tends to mean that they have characterless woodwork and wrought iron light fittings. You might prefer to call them austere or spartan: more suitable for a monastic retreat, and certainly less than you would expect from this class of hotel. Most have views of either the courtyard or the garden, and the grand mountains beyond.

Nearby Monastery church (next door).

28741, El Paular, Rascafría Madrid
Tel (91) 869 1011
Fax (91) 869 1006
Location in mountains of Sierra de Guadarrama, near village; with garden and car parking
Meals breakfast, lunch, dinner
Prices rooms PP-PPPP; breakfast PP; meals PP
Rooms 36 double, all with bath; 17 single, 2 with bath, 15 with shower; 5 suites, all with bath; all rooms have central heating, phone, TV
Facilities 2 dining-rooms, sitting-room, bar, games room; swimming-pool, tennis courts, mountain bikes **Credit cards** AE, DC, V **Children** welcome; under 12s free; special play area **Disabled** access difficult **Pets** accepted if small
Closed never
Manager Manuel Iruela

Guadalajara

Castle Parador, Sigüenza

PT Castillo de Sigüenza

Other castles seem small in comparison with this massive example, which stands defiantly alone on a hill above the town that it guards, at the top of a steep cobbled street.

Unfortunately, the most interesting bits – the towers and battlements – are out of bounds. But there is plenty left to explore. Near Room 239, for example, an inconspicuous slit in the wall leads to a secret balcony high over the silent 13thC Romanesque chapel.

The sitting-room ('the throne room'), held up by six stone pillars and containing two fireplaces, is big enough for giants to repose in, and is sprinkled with regal chairs crowned with gold knobs. The layout is rather formal, in contrast to the inviting stone-arched bar, with its benches and leather chairs.

The bedrooms come with or without overhanging wooden balconies overlooking the large courtyard, with its ornamental hedges and soothingly gurgling fountain, but one balcony (Room 210) dangles daringly over the castle's outer walls. Twelve rooms now have four-poster beds. The walls between rooms are not all of fortress proportions; we found that the noise of other guests' televisions, plumbing and conversations travelled easily.
Nearby Roman arch at Medinacelli (20 km), Atienza (30 km).

Plaza del Castillo, 19250, Sigüenza, Guadalajara
Tel (949) 390100
Location on hill overlooking town, at top of steep cobbled street; with car park
Meals breakfast, lunch, dinner
Prices rooms PPP-PPPP, breakfast P; meals PP
Rooms 76 double, 3 single, 2 family rooms, all with bath; all rooms have central heating, air-conditioning, phone,

TV, minibar
Facilities dining-room, sitting-room, bar, patio; gymnasium
Credit cards AE, DC, MC, V
Children welcome
Disabled access easy; lift/elevator
Pets not accepted
Closed never
Manager Juan Carlos Sánchez

Toledo

Country house hotel, Toledo

La Almazara

Just a few kilometres out of Toledo is this hotel on a wooded hill-top overlooking the city. The views are magnificent –and cost half the price of the Parador further around the hill. It is a simple, rustic place, built as a country residence in the 16thC. A gravel courtyard is surrounded on three sides by a solid ivy-clad building; the hotel rooms are on two of these sides, while the owner's home forms the third.

This is not the sort of place you would want to lounge around in all day, and it does not have a restaurant, but it is the perfect haven after a hot day's sightseeing in touristy Toledo. The staff are friendly and the atmosphere is very laid back. The huge sitting-room looks lived in – comfy sofas around a log fire, piles of magazines and books scattered on tables, and a TV in one corner. Breakfast is served in a delightful arched room that leads on to a small (and rather overgrown) terrace. All the bedrooms are simple, cool and spacious (extra beds can be installed), and are brightened up by locally-made curtains and bedspreads. Bedrooms 1 to 9 all have balconies overlooking Toledo but they need to be booked in advance.

Nearby Toledo – Alcázar, cathedral, El Greco museum, synagogue and Jewish quarter; Madrid (70 km).

Ctra Toledo-Arges km 3.4, 48080, Toledo
Tel (925) 223866
Fax (925) 250562
Location on hill overlooking Toledo; 3 km from Carretera Circunvalación, on Cuerva road; with car parking in courtyard
Meals breakfast
Prices rooms P-PP; breakfast P
Rooms 18 double, 2 single, one family room, all with bath; all rooms have central heating, phone
Facilities sitting-room, breakfast room
Credit cards AE, DC, MC, V
Children welcome
Disabled 6 ground-floor rooms
Pets not accepted
Closed Nov to mid-Mar
Manager Paulino Villamor

Toledo

Town mansion, Toledo

Hostal del Cardenal

This classy little hotel was one of the highlights of our last inspection tour. It occupies a long, pale-brick mansion, built in the 18thC as the summer residence of the archbishop of Toledo, Cardinal Lorenzana. It is set in beautiful shaded gardens, virtually enclosed by the old city walls, rising in three tiers to an impressive, crested doorway. The lowest tier of the garden incorporates an excellent restaurant, now run independently but used by all the guests.

Every room oozes style and character; the sitting-rooms contain well-chosen antiques, the stairway has a beautiful sculpted ceiling, bedrooms have old painted-wood bedheads, and bathrooms have hand-painted tiles and old mirrors. There is a clever mixture of old and new throughout; original Moorish corbels support beams in the upstairs corridor, while modern Moorish sculpture surrounds bedroom doors downstairs. There are two brick courtyards, decorated with ferns, terracotta pots and lilies.

This is a magical place to enjoy a warm summer's evening. You need to book well in advance as it is extremely popular, especially with British and American tourists.

Nearby Alcázar, cathedral, El Greco Museum, synagogue and Jewish quarter; Madrid (70 km).

Paseo de Recaredo 24, 45004, Toledo
Tel (925) 224900
Fax (925) 222991
E-mail Cardenal@macom.es
Location within city walls near main gate (Puerta de Bisagra); with garden but no private car parking
Meals breakfast; lunch and dinner in adjacent restaurant of same name
Prices rooms PP-PPPP; breakfast P; dinner in restaurant PP
Rooms 22 double, 3 single, 2 suites, all with bath; all rooms have central heating, phone; most have air-conditioning, hairdrier, TV
Facilities breakfast room, 2 sitting-rooms
Credit cards AE, DC, MC, V
Children welcome
Disabled no special facilities
Pets accepted **Closed** never
Proprietor Luis González

Toledo

Town hotel, Toledo

Pintor El Greco

You could hardly be closer to the sights of Toledo than in this converted and extended 17th century house in the former Jewish quarter of the city.

Behind the original façade, most of the building is modern but the widespread use of sand-blasted pine, wrought iron and Spanish ceramics preserves the historical feel while allowing light, space and all modern comforts.

You can get a feel of the original building by taking the short flight of steps beside Room 3 (which has a brick arch in its bathroom) down to the entrance of a blocked tunnel which once linked the house to the palace behind, and indeed to the city at large.

Some of the bedrooms overlook the square and gardens in front of the hotel and two of the rooms have views of the hillside across the river. There are six secluded rooms in the attic, two of them large family rooms.

If all the hotel lacks is a dining-room, there are plenty of restaurants close by and the owners have their own beyond the city walls.

Prices increase for Toledo's Holy Week celebrations.

Nearby El Greco museum, El Tránsito synagogue, cathedral.

Alamillos del Tránsito, 13,
45002 Toledo
Tel (925) 214250
Fax (925) 215819
Location next to El Greco
museum; no car parking
Meals breakfast
Prices rooms PP; breakfast P
Rooms 33 double, one single,
all with bath; all rooms have
central heating, air-conditioning, TV, minibar, telephone,
safe, hairdrier

Facilities sitting-room,
breakfast room
Credit cards AE, DC, MC, V
Children accepted
Disabled ramp available, lift
to 2nd floor
Pets accepted
Closed never
Manager Mariano Sánchez

Cuenca

Country hotel, Cuenca

Hotel La Cueva del Fraile

Set in the same green, high-walled valley as the city of Cuenca, this is a larger hotel than at first it appears to be, and the 16thC ancestry to which it lays claim is scarcely in evidence, for all its blackened beams. But the hotel, gathered around a brilliant-white courtyard, does have many other virtues.

There is a great variety of public rooms on the ground floor taking in numerous seating areas and a rather gloomy bar with comfortable settees. There is also a good choice of activities, including a pool and tennis court, and bicycles for hire. The hotel has a children's play area. The bedrooms are divided into the old, the new and the very new. In almost all of them the 'old' wooden beams of the ceiling clash with the new white wood of the doors and cupboards. If you want something special, room 130 is a tasteful suite with a cottage-style sitting room and rocking chairs.

The hotel makes an excellent base for excursions to Cuenca and its scenic surroundings. Ask Fernando on reception for the best places to go: he is the co-author of one of the best guide books to the area.

Nearby Cuenca; Ventano del Diablo (30 km); Ciudad Encantada (45 km).

Carretera de Buenache, Hoz del río Húecar, 16001, Cuenca **Tel** (969) 211571 **Fax** (969) 256047 **Location** in gorge of river Húecar, 7 km from Cuenca on Buenache road; with garden and car parking **Meals** breakfast, lunch, dinner **Prices** rooms PP-PPPP; breakfast P; meals PP **Rooms** 56 double, 4 single, one suite, 2 family rooms, all with bath; all have central heating, phone, hairdrier, TV **Facilities** 3 dining-rooms, 4 sitting-rooms, bar, billiards, dance floor; swimming-pool, tennis court **Credit cards** AE, DC, MC, V **Children** welcome; play area; baby-sitting **Disabled** access possible; 8 ground-floor rooms **Pets** not accepted **Closed** Jan and Feb **Proprietor** Francisco de Borja García

Cuenca

Town house hotel, Cuenca

Posada de San José

Once the home of the in-laws of Velazquez's daughter and later a cathedral choir school, this Posada could hardly offer better credentials. Today – with a 1961 addition – it is a six-tier labyrinth replete with curios, antique furniture and even frescoes. If you like stairs, antiques, history and exploring, this is the hotel for you.

Jennifer Morter, an expatriate Canadian, and her Spanish husband Antonio have lovingly decorated every room with great attention to detail and cleanliness ('you could sit on the floor', Jennifer likes to say). The sheets are pressed and turned back in the old-fashioned way. The 30 rooms are all different and each has been given individual character – you may get a four-poster bed, a Latin inscription on the wall or a dreamy balcony with a magnificent view across the valley. Room 33 is the most popular, with its sloping floor and two balconies.

The rooms themselves are cosy enough to sit in but there is also a rambling breakfast room and bar where tapas is served, with intimate nooks and a sunny terrace, a TV room stranded on its own peculiar floor and a hall with a few antiques and a sofa.

Nearby Cathedral and Casas Colgadas (both within a short walk); Ventano del Diablo (25 km), Ciudad Encantada (35 km).

Calle Julian Romero 4, 16001, Cuenca
Tel (969) 211300
Fax (969) 230365
Location off Plaza Mayor in old part of town, down narrow road past cathedral; no private car parking
Meals breakfast
Prices rooms P-PP; breakfast P; meals PP
Rooms 17 double, 12 with bath; 5 single, 2 with shower;
8 family rooms, 7 with bath; all rooms have central heating
Facilities breakfast room, TV room, bar
Credit cards AE,DC, V
Children welcome
Disabled access difficult
Pets accepted in bedrooms
Closed never; bar only, Mon
Proprietor Jennifer Morter and Antonio Cortinas

Cuenca

Castle Parador, Alarcón

PT Marqués de Villena

You may not believe your eyes as you approach Alarcón, so improbable is the position of the castle which has guarded the village since Moorish times – overlooking the valley of the deep-green Río Júcar, on the edge of Don Quixote's La Mancha.

You may feel like a wandering knight returning from the Crusades as you step into the quaint little courtyard with its well in the middle. Within the thick castle walls you should sleep well and live in typical Parador style, with your minibar discreetly hidden in a reproduction antique cabinet; the pick of the bedrooms is number 103, with a canopied bed and steps up to a high window where distressed damsels might sit and dream of rescue. The sitting-room-cum-cafeteria has everything you could want of a great hall: a circular iron chandelier, an enormous tapestry depicting a coat of arms, a suit of armour and three wooden thrones. The dining-room is also a vaulted chamber, with a long slit window.

A lift will whisk you up to the battlements for a view worthy of a feudal baron. The village has several other historical buildings and there are some good walks.

Nearby Castle of Belmonte (70 km), Mota del Cuervo (85 km) and Cuenca (85 km).

Avenida Amigos del Castillo, 16213, Alarcón, Cuenca
Tel (969) 331350
Fax (969) 330303
Location on huge rock encircled by river, at end of village; car parking outside castle
Meals breakfast, lunch, dinner
Prices rooms PPPP; breakfast P; meals PP
Rooms 12 double, one single, all with bath; all rooms have central heating, phone,

TV, minibar
Facilities dining-room, sitting-room, bar
Credit cards AE, DC, MC, V
Children welcome; special play area
Disabled access difficult; lift/ elevator
Pets not accepted
Closed never
Manager Aurora Lozano

Cuenca

Town hotel, Mota del Cuervo

Mesón de Don Quijote

If Don Quixote himself was not to be taken too seriously, then neither is his *mesón*, which is inauspiciously located behind a petrol station in a little town overlooked by windmills in the heart of La Mancha.

The whole ground floor - with its cartwheel chandeliers, theatrical staircase, papier-maché well and cobbled inn-courtyard-cum-lounge (where the ingenious hidalgo could easily have been knighted) – flirts with the memory of Cervantes' hero. All that is lacking is the buxom Dulcinea. Fixtures and fittings are typically 'rustic' and Castilian – history as it never was. The chunky dining-room chairs, all nuts and bolts, must have been a fascinating woodwork project for somebody. The bar-stools are reminiscent of something out of a medieval torture chamber.

The waiters are dressed in 'traditional' costume, with broad red cummerbunds, grey waistcoats and bootlace ties. The restaurant's excellent menu includes a hearty vegetarian bean soup and home-made rice pudding.

Unfortunately, the rustic illusion stops short of the bedrooms, which are fairly nondescript. But the rest of the hotel should keep you well entertained.

Nearby Belmonte Castle (15 km); El Toboso (15 km).

Francisco Costi 2, 16630, Mota del Cuervo, Cuenca
Tel (969) 180200
Location behind filling station on main road through town; with car parking
Meals breakfast, lunch, dinner
Prices rooms P-PP; breakfast P; meals PP
Rooms 28 double, 7 single, one suite, all with bath; all rooms have central heating, air-conditioning, phone
Facilities dining-room, 3 sitting-rooms, bar; swimming-pool
Credit cards AE, DC, MC, V
Children accepted
Disabled access difficult
Pets not accepted
Closed never
Proprietor José María Palacios

Ciudad Real

Converted convent Parador, Almagro

PT de Almagro

Almagro's Parador has ancient origins (it is on the site of a 16thC Franciscan convent) but is almost entirely modern, built just a decade ago. The layout of the building is highly unusual – the rooms are set around fourteen little quads, all different from each other. The first one you come to has ivy-clad walls and fig trees shading a small fountain, the second bamboo trees around a pond, the third rose-bushes, and so on.

It would be easy to get lost inside – every corridor looks the same – if it were not for the lovely hand-painted signs and room numbers on every corner. Such attention to detail runs throughout – there are painted ceilings and bright tapestries in the public rooms, tiled bed-heads and locally made lace covers in the bedrooms, and fresh flowers throughout. The *bodega* is built on two floors in the old cellars of the convent; massive storage jars go up through the floor and are used as table tops on the upper level. Other cosy sitting-rooms are dotted about.

Despite its size, this is one of the friendliest Paradors – an interesting place in a picturesque town on the plains of Don Quixote's La Mancha.

Nearby Plaza Mayor, old town, lace-making; Ciudad Real (25 km); Valdepeñas (35 km).

Ronda de San Francisco, 13270, Almagro, Ciudad Real
Tel (926) 860100
Fax (926) 860150
Location in quiet street, near centre of town, signed from main road; with garden and car parking
Meals breakfast, lunch, dinner
Prices rooms PP-PPPP; breakfast P; meals PP
Rooms 48 double, 6 single, one suite; all with bath; all rooms have central heating, air-conditioning, phone, TV, minibar
Facilities 2 dining-rooms, 2 sitting-rooms, bar, terrace; swimming-pool
Credit cards AE, DC, MC, V
Children welcome
Disabled access easy
Pets not accepted
Closed never
Manager José Maria Lopez de Santos

Teruel

Converted tower house, Valderobbres

Torre del Visco

New to this latest edition of the guide, Torre del Visco is a remote 15thC semi-fortified estate house which has been carefully restored by its English owners, Piers and Jemma Markham, who have lived in Spain for many years. This is a real hideaway: the nearest villages are 7.5 miles (12 km) away, and the hotel is reached by car-friendly forest tracks. Arriving at the final turn in the track, you see at last the lovely outlines of the house, surrounded by 200 acres of farmland. Standing on a steep hillside overlooking the beautiful valley of the river Tastavins, it is a haven of peace, with a warm welcome from the owners. You can walk, ride or mountain bike along the valley or up into the mountains, followed by rest and relaxation on the terrace, in the sitting-room with its grand piano and open fire, or in the well-stocked library. Breakfast is taken in the farmhouse kitchen, while dinner features Mediterranean cuisine using produce from the farm as well as fish bought directly from the quayside. The white-walled bedrooms are simple and fresh, with tiled floors, and the whole place feels like a home, not a hotel. All the rooms enjoy superb views across the untamed landscape.

Nearby Valderrobres, 7.5 miles (12 km); Morella, 33 miles (53 km).

Apartado 15, 44580 Valderrobres, Teruel
Tel (978) 769015
Fax (978) 769016
Location 7.5 miles (12 km) S of Valderrobres; hotel signposted after 3.5 miles (6 km); in own farmland with ample parking
Meals breakfast, lunch, dinner
Prices rooms PPP-PPPP; dinner (obligatory) PPP
Rooms 8 double, 4 suites, all with bath; all rooms have central heating, hairdrier
Facilities 3 sitting rooms, dining room, library, *bodega*, terrace, gardens
Credit cards MC, V
Children accepted
Disabled access difficult
Pets not accepted
Closed Jan 7-24

Teruel

Fonda Guimerá

Take a walled medieval village – complete with watch-tower, numerous Gothic palaces and wide cobbled streets – restore all these elements carefully, and what you have is Mirambel, once acclaimed the 'most beautiful village in Spain' by Queen Sofía.

The old *fonda* has also been restored. Its façade on the main street is in keeping with the rest of this historic village but everything behind it is ultra-new. All the bedrooms are modern and comfortable. Although half provide nothing more than basic accommodation, those at the back of the building have small bathrooms and balconies, and the central heating is needed in winter.

The Fonda is a simple, inexpensive place to stay and it does not have a sitting-room or any other public facilities. But you can always have a drink with the locals in the small, gloomy public bar next door which doubles as reception (don't be put off by its appearance), and with a restaurant behind.

The village itself is a fascinating place to stroll around and is set in magnificent countryside, reminiscent of the Yorkshire Dales, which is good for walking and cycling. It is still just off the beaten tourist track, and worth the detour.

Nearby Cantavieja (15 km), Morella (30 km).

Calle Agustín Pastor 28, 44141, Mirambel, Teruel
Tel (964) 178269
Fax (964) 178293
Location on cobbled street in village; no private car parking
Meals breakfast, lunch, dinner
Prices rooms P; breakfast P; meals P
Rooms 18 double, 8 with bath; some rooms have central heating
Facilities dining-room, bar
Credit cards V
Children welcome
Disabled access difficult
Pets not accepted
Closed never
Manager Pedro Guimerá

Teruel

Castle Parador, Alcañiz

PT La Concordia

Still dominating the town and its green river from the summit of a hill, as it has done since the 12th century, this castle-monastery is the first thing that you see as you approach Alcañiz; it certainly looks too big to have only 12 rooms.

Although monumental in scale, the former home of the Order of the Knights of Calatrava has been converted into an intimate hotel full of historical character. It is furnished in a modern imitation of castle-style, with wrought iron chandeliers everywhere and gold knobs topping the chairs in a dining-room fit for medieval banquets. In the bedrooms, however, you can forget that you are in a castle, as evidence of the past has been largely crowded out by new furnishings. There are magnificent views from most of the rooms and the rest look on to the peaceful cloister-garden behind.

The castle is also a tourist attraction and its grounds are open to the public – so it is not a place in which to seek seclusion. The TV in the cafeteria at the entrance, in an elegant vaulted chamber, sometimes intrudes too, but at night the castle returns more or less to its ancestral peace.

Nearby Caspe (30 km) – Roman temple, caves of Molinos (40 km), El Parrisal near Beceite (50 km) – wildlife.

Castillo de los Calatravos, 44600, Alcañiz, Teruel
Tel (978) 830400
Location on hill dominating town (follow Parador signs); with garden and car parking
Meals breakfast, lunch, dinner
Prices rooms PPPP; breakfast P; meals PP
Rooms 10 double, 2 single, all with bath; all rooms have central heating, air-conditioning, phone,
TV, minibar
Facilities 2 dining-rooms, 2 sitting-rooms, cafeteria
Credit cards AE, DC, MC, V
Children welcome
Disabled access easy; lift/elevator
Pets not accepted
Closed 18 Dec to 1 Feb
Manager Miguel Cruz

Castellón

Converted palace, Morella

Hotel Cardenal Ram

Cardinal Ram's 16thC Gothic palace, set in a commanding position on Morella's medieval porticoed main street, is a local landmark. Its thick walls enclose a variety of spacious rooms. The furnishings have seen better days and do not accord with the age and style of the building, and the beds tend to be too soft for comfort. But the bathrooms are modern and well-equipped, and the rooms on the 2nd and 3rd floors have magnificent views.

The excellent restaurant is well known for its local delicacies including the succulent *cordero trufado* – lamb stuffed with truffles – the hearty Morella soup and *tarta al whisky* – home-made ice-cream. (It is only fair to advise you that you can get the same fare at lower prices just down the road in another restaurant, Casa Roque, under the same management as Cardenal Ram.) The hotel breakfast, it must be said, is disappointingly ordinary even by Spanish standards.

The hotel lacks seating and recreational space, but it makes up for this with its age and character. It is arguably overpriced for the level of comfort offered, but you can eat well here and it is as close to the authentic history of Morella as you will get.

Nearby Castle and church; La Balma (25 km), Montalvana –cave paintings (25 km), Mirambel (30 km) – walled village.

Cuesta Suñer 1, 12300,
Morella, Castellón
Tel (964) 160000
Location in heart of Morella,
on main street; no private
car parking
Meals breakfast, lunch, dinner
Prices rooms P-PP; breakfast
P; dinner PP
Rooms 18 double, 1 single,
all with bath; all rooms have
central heating, phone, TV
Facilities dining-room,

hall/sitting-room
Credit cards AE, DC, MC, V
Children welcome
Disabled access difficult
Pets not accepted
Closed never
Proprietor Roque Gutierrez

Castellón

Hostal Elías

Centrally located within the walls of the magnificent medieval hill-top town of Morella, Hostal Elías occupies a tastefully modernised town house, sparkling clean and excellent value.

All the rooms vary slightly but most of them are large. Some have small entrance halls separating the bathroom from the bedroom; others small sitting-rooms; and most of them have thin balconies looking over a picturesque street and catching the morning or evening sun. The wooden furniture is simple, and of varying antiquity and attractiveness – but it is always adequate, with plenty of storage. Rooms at the top of the building, although smaller, are cosy and have wonderful views.

Señor Elías is quiet but a very friendly man and a mine of information to be plundered when the tourist office is closed (which it seems to be for much of the year).

Although Hostal Elías does not serve food, a short walk brings you to Morella's main street, which has several bars and restaurants, including the excellent Casa Roque – owned by the same people as the Cardenal Ram (page 128).

Nearby La Balma (25 km), Montalvana (35 km) – cave paintings, Mirambel (30 km) – walled village.

Calle Colomer 7, 12300, Morella, Castellón
Tel (964) 160092
Location in front of church on corner of two quiet streets; no private car parking
Meals not available
Prices rooms P
Rooms 16 double, one single, all with bath; all rooms have central heating
Facilities sitting-room, TV room

Credit cards not accepted
Children welcome
Disabled access easy; 4 ground-floor rooms
Pets accepted
Closed 15 days in autumn
Proprietor Elias and Palmira Antoli

Valencia

Hotels in Valencia

Valencia, Spain's third largest city, is relatively little-visited by tourists. Its international fame rests mainly on paella. In Spain it is also known for its nightlife (facilitated by year-round balmy temperatures), its prolific production of oranges and the spectacular Fallas fiesta in March during which huge papier mâché monuments are burnt in the streets. It is the capital of a large region on the eastern seaboard, including numerous cultural tourist attractions still undiscovered by the hordes.

Most of the city's hotels cater predominantly for trade fair and business visitors. The best are a long way out of town. The purpose-built seaside Parador, Luis Vives (Tel (96) 161 1186), is on the edge of a nature reserve and surrounded by a golf course. Nearby is another modern hotel, the Sidi Saler Palace (Tel (96) 161 0411). The luxurious 82-room Monte Picayo (Tel (96) 142 0100), the choice of VIPs, is a short way inland, (conveniently close to the A7 motorway) and has its own casino and adjacent bullring.

In the city centre, apart from the Excelsior (see below), the best of the smaller hotels is probably Hotel Inglés (Tel (96) 351 6426), housed in an old palace. The art nouveau-style Reina Victoria (Tel (96) 352 0487), with 97 rooms, retains an air of the *belle époque* in which it was built. A much larger central hotel is the modern Astoria Palace (Tel (96) 352 6737).

Hotel Excelsior

Handsome, old and mostly refurbished, the Excelsior offers greater comfort and charm than many of Valencia's more expensive hotels. Despite the odd plastic plant, the whole place is imbued with past elegance: the stairs are carpeted, the lift has brass doors and old furniture is scattered here and there. Many of the bedrooms are let down by their small bathrooms with old fittings, but the suites, with their brass bedsteads, painted cornices, floral textiles and cosy ante-rooms, are highly desirable. Away from your room, you have to choose between a noisy bar and a somewhat formal English-style sitting-room.

Nearby Palacio del Marqués de Dos Aguas, Lonja, market.

Calle Barcelonina 5, 46002, Valencia
Tel (96) 3514612
Fax (96) 3523478
Location in middle of town, near Plaza del Ayuntamiento; no private car parking
Meals breakfast, lunch, dinner
Prices rooms PP-PPPP; breakfast P; lunch PP, dinner P
Rooms 38 double, 18 single, 9 family rooms, all with bath; all rooms have central heating, air-conditioning, phone; most rooms have TV
Facilities dining-room, sitting-room, cafeteria
Credit cards AE, DC, MC, V
Children welcome
Disabled easy access; lift/elevator
Pets not accepted
Closed never
Manager Roberto Plá

Alicante

Roadside inn, Calpe

Venta La Chata

It is easy to imagine coaches drawing up at this old inn a hundred years ago to change horses and set down passengers for the night. Since then it has been restored and partly modernized, keeping the old flavour but adding some of the comforts that modern travellers expect.

The rooms are varied, mixing old and new furniture in a piecemeal assortment. Most of the bathrooms have ageing fittings. Ask for a room with a terrace-suntrap overlooking the leafy, peaceful garden. Some of the rooms also have views of Calpe's Gibraltar-like rock, the Peñón de Ifach.

Downstairs there are informal tables in the breakfast/TV room in front of reception and more inviting chairs and tables on the two terraces and under the arches of the entrance porch. The cool, open-plan sitting-room, decorated with old pots, gourds and an enormous gold-framed mirror, has some cosy armchairs. The restaurant, popular with non-residents, is lit by a long line of windows and has a door leading into the garden. Among the cactuses, clumps of bamboo and flowers that gather around a mature carob tree, there are some quiet, shady corners.
Nearby Calpe (5 km), Peñón de Ifach (10km), Altea (15 km), Jávea (25 km), Castell de Guadalest (35 km).

Carretera Nacional 332 km 172, 03710, Calpe, Alicante
Tel (96) 583 0308
Location on main N332 (Valencia to Alicante), 4 km north of Calpe; with garden and car parking
Meals breakfast
Prices rooms P; breakfast P
Rooms 16 double, one single, all with bath; all rooms have TV, phone
Facilities dining-room, 2 sitting-rooms, terrace; tennis court
Credit cards AE, DC, V
Children welcome; play area in garden
Disabled access difficult
Pets accepted
Closed never
Proprietor María Giner

Alicante

Beach hotel, Denia

Rosa

Denia, with its balmy Mediterranean climate, won the heart of Michel Kessous, Parisian by birth and globetrotter by inclination, who arrived on holiday at the beginning of the 1970s and still has not moved on. His hard work and optimism have brought about the conversion of the humble pension, which he built, into a handsome villa with colonnaded façade and Florentine-style balconies.

The bedrooms in the main house are somewhat narrow and have recently been redecorated and equipped in the manner of a grand hotel; the self-catering bungalows are more suitable for a holiday with children or for a long stay.

Nearby Denia castle (1 km); Les Rotes beach (4 km).

Congre 3, Las Marinas, 03700, Denia, Alicante
Tel (96) 5781573
Fax (96) 6424774
Location off the coast road; garden and car parking
Meals breakfast, lunch, dinner
Prices rooms PP-PPP; breakfast P; meals PP
Rooms 34 double, 1 single, 5 small suites, all with bath; all rooms have central heating, air conditioning, phone, safe, satellite TV, hairdrier
Facilities dining-room, bar, terrace; swimming-pool, tennis court, table tennis **Credit cards** MC, V **Children** very welcome; playground and paddling pool **Disabled** access easy; some specially equipped rooms **Pets** accepted
Closed Nov to Mar
Proprietor Michel Kessous

Seaside resort hotel, Moraira

Swiss Hotel Moraira

The Swiss watches on sale in the lobby and the private hair salon set the tone for this hotel which goes for luxury at the expense of personality.

Set in an estate of holiday villas a short way back from the coast, its central feature is the large swimming-pool surrounded by a sun-trapping terrace onto which all rooms have views and more or less direct access. The bedrooms are spacious, especially the 'semi-suites' and suites, and lavishly equipped – all newly furnished, although in predictable grand hotel style. The staff are discreet and faultlessly formal.

Nearby Peñón de Ifach (12km); Jávea (14km); Jalón Valley.

Urbanización Club Moraira, 03724, Moraira, Alicante
Tel (96) 5747104
Fax (96) 5747074
Location 1.5km from Moraira (signposted off Calpe road)
Meals breakfast, lunch, dinner
Prices rooms PPP-PPPP; breakfast P; meals PP
Rooms 18 double, 5 semi-suites, 2 suites, all with bath; all rooms have central heating, air-conditioning, TV, minibar, telephone
Facilities dining-room, sitting-room, bar, swimming-pool
Credit cards AE, DC, MC, V
Children accepted
Disabled easy access
Pets accepted at extra charge
Closed never
Manager Santiago Bravo

Alicante

City hotel, Elche

Huerto del Cura

This hotel – like the whole city of Elche – lies in the welcome shade of the most extensive palm groves in Europe. The Mediterranean-style houses, into which it is divided, are deliberately lower than the palm fronds. Add the swimming-pool and the tropical plants in the hotel grounds and the effect is of a secluded, exclusive, Saharan oasis – a relief after the concrete blocks which pass for hotels on the nearby Costa Blanca. 'Everything was excellent', reported the owner of a hotel featured in our British guide, who stayed here recently.

The hotel is a *Parador colaborador*, meaning that it shares some of the marketing arrangements of the state-run chain. You can expect a similarly high quality of service. The owner, José Orts, spares no effort in keeping his hotel up to scratch – some suites come with whirlpool baths; others have computers connected to the Internet. The chef of Els Capellans restaurant offers regional and French dishes. In summer, you can dine by the swimming-pool on lamb chops with basil and date-flavoured crème caramel.

Directly across the road is the Huerto de Cura (Priest's Garden), with a reproduction of the Dama de Elche Iberian statue.
Nearby La Alcudia archaeological museum; Laguna del Hondo wildlife reserve (7 km); trips to Tabarca Isle.

Porta de la Morena, 14,
03202, Elche, Alicante
Tel (96) 5458040
Fax (96) 5421910
Location Elche, Huerto del Cura gardens; garden and car parking
Meals breakfast, lunch, dinner
Prices rooms PP-PPPP; breakfast P; meals PP
Rooms 69 double, 7 single, 4 family rooms, all with bath; all rooms have air-conditioning, telephone, minibar, radio, TV, hairdrier
Facilities restaurant, cafeteria, meeting room; terrace, sitting-room, swimming-pool, tennis court; gymnasium, sauna **Credit cards** AE, DC, MC, V **Children** welcome
Disabled many facilities; rooms in bungalows
Pets not accepted
Closed never
Proprietor José Orts

Alicante

Pensión Castells

Having converted an old village house and found themselves with a surplus of rooms, Jan and Eric Wright decided to put them to profitable use. Many of their guests come to walk in the surrounding mountains, guided by Eric.

From the street you step directly into the sitting-cum-dining-room. At the window end, by the street door, is the table around which everyone eats Jan's home cooking together. At the other end comfy armchairs are arranged by the hearth. Upstairs are four simple but cosy rooms, each a different shape; all of them furnished with a loving touch. Two of them have sloping beamed roofs. The top one, dubbed 'the Casita', is the favourite: by the bed are a shelf of books and a tea-maker. The staircase ends in a sunny terrace at rooftop level.

Although Castell de Castells is not far from the Costa Blanca it gets few tourists and the principal attraction is rural peace. The Wrights warn potential visitors that there is little for children to do in the area. If you don't mind sharing your table with whoever else happens to be staying, this is one definition of the charming small hotel.

Nearby natural rock arches (5km); Jalon valley vineyards (20km); Castell de Guadalest (33km); Costa Blanca (35km).

Calle San Vicente 18, 03793, Castell de Castells, Alicante
Tel (96) 5518254
Location in a narrow street in the centre of the village: park near the church and ask for directions.
Meals breakfast, dinner
Prices rooms PP; Continental breakfast P, English breakfast P; dinner PP
Rooms 3 twin, one double, all with shower and toilet; all rooms have central heating
Facilities sitting/dining-room
Credit cards none
Children accepted
Disabled access difficult
Pets not accepted
Closed Jul and Aug
Proprietors Eric and Jan Wright

Murcia

Hotel Termas

The oldest and most attractive of the three hotels in a leafy spa founded by the Romans, the Termas is decorated inside in a superb Mozarabic style. With its cupolas, patios and ornate plasterwork, at times you could believe that you were staying in the Alhambra. Most guests come for the waters, and there is a rest-cure calm in the sitting-room with its coffered ceiling and card tables. The bedrooms are pleasantly modern, some of them looking through eucalyptus trees to the river. Two floors down is a labyrinth of humid tunnels heated by warm water which gushes out of the ground.

Nearby Murcia (25 km); Alcantarilla waterwheel (30 km).

Balneario de Archena, 30600, Archena, Murcia
Tel (968) 670100
Location by river Segura, through town (follow signs); with grounds and car parking
Meals breakfast, lunch, dinner
Prices rooms PP-PPP; breakfast P; meals PP
Rooms 60 double, 10 single, all with bath; all have central heating, air-conditioning, phone, TV, minibar, radio
Facilities dining-room, sitting-room; spa; swimming-pool, 2 tennis courts
Credit cards accepted
Children welcome
Disabled easy access; lift/elevator
Pets not accepted
Closed never
Manager Mercedes Coghen

Paradores in Eastern Spain

The Paradores on the east coast of Spain are modern and functional, with little charm. The PT Costa del Azahar at Benicarlo is a box-like building (108 rooms) set in beautiful gardens facing 6 km of gently curving beach (Tel (964) 470100). Just south of Valencia, on the narrow sandy peninsula of El Saler is the PT Luis Vives, a golf hotel with its own 18-hole course (Tel (96) 161 1186). Further down the coast on the Javea peninsula is another unremarkable 1960s creation, the 65-room PT Costa Blanca (Tel (96) 5790200). The PT de Puerto Lumbreras, 80 km SW of Murcia, is not on the coast, despite its maritime-sounding name. It is a plain but smart white hotel (60 rooms) on the main road through the town. Its floors are chequered marble, and the walls are brightened up by local ceramics (Tel (96) 8402025)

Of the places further inland, only the PT La Concordia at Alcañiz (a hilltop castle with just 12 rooms) gets a full entry here (see page 127). The PT de Teruel is a modern hotel overlooking the city which is famous for its integration of Christian, Jewish and Muslim styles of architecture (Tel (974) 602553). The PT de la Mancha, south of Albacete, is a low, white building on the sprawling plains of La Mancha. It is decorated in rustic style with beamed ceilings and primitive wooden farm tools hanging from the walls – donkey baskets, oxen yokes, ploughshares (Tel (967) 229450).

Huelva

Country hotel, Los Marines

Finca Buenvino

As our inspectors discovered, this is not an easy place to find; the lovely modern villa, built in 18thC style on the top of a hill, is hidden away in the heart of a National Park, amid chestnut forests, fruit trees and bubbling springs.

Sam and Jeannie Chesterton, an English couple, stress that this is their home and that you are expected to join in with the family (who are very easy-going). Everyone eats together – on the terrace in summer or in the panelled dining-room. Jeannie is a trained cordon bleu cook, and produces mouth-watering dinners and salad lunches, accompanied by liberal amounts of wine. Drinks taken at other times – and perhaps consumed before the huge fireplace of the sitting-room or in the airy conservatory – are recorded in an 'honesty book'.

The bedrooms are all bright and comfortable. The two attic rooms have hand-stencilled walls and wonderful views over the woods. The other two rooms are smaller and share a bathroom. The Chestertons are planning to restore the cottages on their land for further guests, who will also dine at the house and have use of the swimming-pool, spectacularly perched above the house.

Nearby Aracena (caves and castle); Zafra (85 km).

21293, Los Marines, Huelva
Tel (959) 124034
Location in heart of woodland, off N433 W of Los Marines, itself W of Aracena; with garden and shaded car parking
Meals breakfast, lunch, dinner
Prices DB&B PPP
Rooms 4 double, all with bath; all rooms have central heating, hairdrier, kettle
Facilities dining-room, sitting-room, TV room, conservatory; swimming-pool
Credit cards AE, DC, MC, V
Children welcome; play facilities
Disabled access difficult
Pets not accepted
Closed check by phone before visiting
Proprietors Sam and Jeannie Chesterton

Huelva

Town hotel, Aracena

Sierra de Aracena

The attractive town of Aracena is built in tiers on a hillside crowned by the remains of a Templar castle. Beneath it, underground rivers have carved out vast narrow caves full of spectacular formations, coloured red by iron oxide – well worth exploring if you are passing through the region.

The Sierra de Aracena, in the wide, cobbled Gran Vía, makes a good base for an overnight stay. It is a solid, square building with an elaborate brick-patterned façade and arches around the ground-floor windows. It is a quiet, sleepy hotel, where the world drifts by without intruding; a few locals may wander in to watch the TV. The sitting-room is pleasantly furnished with wicker chairs, floral fabrics and tiled pictures, and adjoins a modern bar (which doubles as a breakfast room). There is an open fire in winter.

The bedrooms are simple and comfortable. The ones at the back have great views of the castle and Aracena's winding streets and red-tiled roofs. They are all kept spotlessly clean by the friendly staff, who don't speak a word of English but seldom stop smiling. There is no dining-room but several recommended restaurants are to be found in the town.

Nearby Cave of Marvels, castle; Zafra (95 km).

Gran Via 21, 21200, Aracena, Huelva
Tel (959) 126175
Tel (959) 126218
Location on quiet wide street in middle of town; with parking for 8 cars
Meals breakfast
Prices rooms P-PP; breakfast P
Rooms 31 double, 10 single, 2 suites, all with bath; all rooms have central heating, phone, radio, TV and minibar

Facilities sitting-room, bar/breakfast area
Credit cards AE, DC, V
Children accepted
Disabled lift/elevator; some ground-floor rooms
Pets not accepted
Closed never
Manager María del Carmen Fernández

Seville

Castle Parador, Carmona

PT Alcázar del Rey Don Pedro

With 65 rooms and conference facilities, this Parador can hardly be described as 'small and charming'. But it merits inclusion because of its superb location on a hill top above the busy walled town of Carmona. The views are breath-taking.

The Moorish fortress that stood here was transformed into a luxury palace by the craftsmen of the Seville Alcázar for the infamous Don Pedro the Cruel. The Parador architects have taken great care to recreate the 'palace' atmosphere, setting elegant Mudejar columns around a pretty internal courtyard and decorating the stonework and floor tiles with the familiar Moorish star pattern. Extensive renovation was also carried out in 1997.

The public rooms are large and comfortable; glass cases of swords and armour and hanging tapestries give them a 'stately home' feel, but on our visit both the sitting-rooms and cavernous dining-room seemed positively animated. Top-floor bedrooms have amazing views over the fertile plains of the Corbones river. The rooms show more attention to detail than the average Parador room (we had great trouble locating the disguised minibar). We welcome reports on the changes.

Nearby Roman remains; Seville (35 km), Ecija (55 km) –palaces and churches; Córdoba (105 km).

41410, Carmona, Seville
Tel (95) 4141010
Fax (95) 4141712
Location on top of hill in Carmona (follow Parador signs); with garden and ample shaded car parking
Meals breakfast, lunch, dinner
Prices rooms PPP-PPPP, breakfast P; meals PP
Rooms 60 double, 3 single, all with bath; all rooms have central heating,
air-conditioning, phone, TV, hairdrier, minibar, radio
Facilities dining-room, 2 sitting-rooms, bar; swimming-pool
Credit cards AE, DC, V
Children welcome
Disabled most rooms are on ground floor
Pets not accepted
Closed never
Manager Benito Montañés

Seville

Historic palace hotel, Carmona

Casa de Carmona

This hotel is housed in a 16thC palace in the heart of Carmona. Built in Andalucian style, with a distinct Mudejar influence, it has a two-storey, porticoed central patio and a delightful interior garden. The sitting-room, with its delicate starry ceiling and period pieces reflected in a large Napoleon III mirror, testifies to the fashion and fine art background of the owners, who have faithfully restored the building and filled it with treasures. The cosy bedrooms, are a touch more modern, with light flowery fabrics and all creature comforts alongside attractive antique furniture. A recent visitor, however, thought it overpriced.

Nearby old town and castle; Roman necropolis; Seville (30 km).

Plaza de Lasso, 1, 41410, Carmona, Sevilla
Tel (95) 4191000
Fax (95) 4190189
E-mail schwabach@casadecarmona.com
Location in one of the most important squares in the city; garden and car parking outside
Meals breakfast, lunch, dinner
Prices rooms PPPP; breakfast PP; meals PP

Rooms 13 double, 18 suites, all with bath; all rooms have air conditioning, telephone, radio, minibar, satellite TV
Facilities sitting-room, dining-room, bar; swimming-pool, mini-gym, sauna
Credit cards AE, DC, MC, V
Children accepted **Disabled** access easy **Pets** accepted
Closed never **Manager** Felipe Guardiola Medina

Reporting to the guide

The *Charming Small Hotel Guides* are greatly strengthened by reports from readers. Please write and tell us about your experiences of small hotels, guest-houses and inns, whether good or bad, whether listed in this edition or not. As well as hotels in Spain, we are interested in hotels in Britain and Ireland, Italy, France, Portugal, Austria, Switzerland, Germany and other European countries, and those in the eastern United States. Particularly helpful reporters earn a free copy of the next edition of the guide concerned. And we are always on the lookout for new recruits to our team of inspectors; some undertake trips especially for inspection purposes, while others combine hotel inspections (at our expense, of course) with their own travels.

Categories and stars

Every hotel in Spain is categorised as either Parador, hotel, apartment hotel, *hostal*, motel or *pensión* and given a star rating. Although stars and categories sometimes provide a guide to price and facilities, they say little about the ambience and quality of service you can expect. Many charming hotels have only one or two stars and more than one four-star hotel has failed to impress our inspectors.

Some hotels in the book style themselves posada, venta, fonda, mesón etc. These names derive from older types of wayside lodging and are no longer official categories.

Seville

Hotel Simon

Don't be put off by the neon sign outside; once inside the white wrought iron gates, you find yourself transported back in time. Behind them is the typical Andalucian courtyard of a beautiful Moorish town house – a perfect place to cool down among the ferns and marble busts after a busy morning's sightseeing in this spectacular city.

Decoration in the hotel is reminiscent of a mosque; the walls are covered in pretty Moorish tiles and gilded mirrors. Glass chandeliers hang down between the slender marble pillars. The stairway and corridors have tiled walls and floors, period furniture and cabinets full of silver. Bedrooms tend to vary in size and quality and are the original rooms of this lovely 18thC house. Some have small balconies looking on to the street, while others are rather small and airless. Bathrooms also vary, but all are spotlessly clean.

The staff are friendly and helpful, and obviously take great pride in this unusual hotel. The Simon has only two disadvantages – it can be noisy inside and there's no car parking immediately outside. But it is possible to park nearby and the hotel could not be more central.

Nearby Cathedral, La Giralda, the Alcázar, Jewish quarter.

García de Vinuesa 19, 41001, Seville
Tel (95) 4226660
Location on small street, just west of cathedral; no private car parking
Meals breakfast
Prices rooms P-PP; breakfast P
Rooms 19 double, 15 with bath, 4 with shower; 5 single with shower; 3 suites with bath; all rooms have central heating, phone, air-conditioning
Facilities dining-room, sitting-room, patio
Credit cards AE, DC, MC, V
Children accepted
Disabled some ground-floor rooms
Pets accepted in bedrooms
Closed never
Manager Francisco Aguayo

Seville

Hotel Doña María

Imagine lying by a swimming-pool which overlooks one of the biggest cathedrals in the world – just one of the perks of staying at the Doña María in the heart of Seville. The hotel is built in an old town house, in a cobbled alley-way off the cathedral square – very convenient for sightseeing, not so convenient for parking, unless you get a space in the underground car park.

The hotel has no dining-room, but serves large buffet breakfasts downstairs, and has two bars – one wood-panelled, adjoining the sitting-room, the other on the roof-terrace (in summer only). The other public rooms are elegant and comfortable – the sitting-room has dark red sofas between brick pillars, the landings are crammed with antiques and portraits, the corridors are lit with blue and white glass lamps; and there is a tiny tropical garden in the middle of the building.

Each bedroom is different, apparently decorated by the Marchioness de San Joaquin herself and named after eminent Sevillian ladies. If possible, ask to see several rooms and choose carefully, as some are disappointing and not cheap. The roof-terrace certainly makes up for it – there are not many places where you get a view of Gothic spires as you swim.

Nearby Cathedral, La Giralda, the Alcázar, Jewish quarter.

Don Remondo 19, 41004, Seville
Tel (95) 422 4990
Fax (95) 422 9546
Location in narrow alley-way, leading from square in front of cathedral; underground parking for 9 cars
Meals breakfast
Prices rooms PPP-PPPP; breakfast P
Rooms 35 double, all with bath; 14 single, 12 with bath, 3 with shower; all rooms have central heating, phone, TV, radio; swimming-pool on roof
Facilities 2 sitting-rooms, bar, breakfast room
Credit cards AE, DC, MC, V
Children welcome
Disabled lift/elevator
Pets accepted in 2 bedrooms
Closed never
Manager Isabel Moreno

Seville

Hotel Murillo

To find the Hotel Murillo you need a good sense of direction and a detailed map; it is lost in the historic Barrio de Santa Cruz, a maze of tiny pedestrian passages behind the Alcázar. From the outside, it is a typical Sevillian town house, painted mustard-yellow and white, with wrought-iron grilles and balconies.

From the inside, it is an extraordinary place, a treasure trove of peculiar objects and antiques. Suits of armour guard the entrance to a long, dim room crammed with furniture –leather sling chairs around carved tables, elaborate screens and glass cabinets along the walls, a sedan chair in front of the bar. The panelled ceiling gives you the feeling that you are in the cabin of a medieval ship. This room serves as a sitting, eating and reception area, and there is another small sitting-room for families or groups.

In contrast, the bedrooms upstairs are rather plain. Second-floor rooms have small balconies looking on to the street, third-floor rooms have arched windows. Furniture is functional and bathrooms small. The room keys are attached to miniature paint pallets, emphasizing the connection with the Sevillian artist Murillo, after whom the hotel is named.

Nearby Cathedral, La Giralda, the Alcázar, Jewish quarter.

Lope de Rueda 7 & 9, 41000, Seville
Tel (95) 421 6095
Location in a maze of tiny streets, north of cathedral, approachable only by foot; garages nearby
Meals breakfast
Prices rooms PP-PPP; breakfast P
Rooms 47 double, all with bath; 10 single, with bath,; all rooms have central heating, air-conditioning, phone
Facilities sitting-room, bar
Credit cards AE, DC, MC, V
Children accepted
Disabled lift/elevator
Pets not accepted
Closed never
Manager Enrique Ysasi

Seville

Andalucian villa, Alcalá de Guadaira

Hotel Oromana

Our inspector had trouble finding the Oromana; it is on a hill opposite the town, in an area (of the same name) which is rapidly being developed for residential purposes, eating into the pine woods that surround the hotel. The tranquillity is not yet lost; a long winding drive takes you away from the building sites to the rounded knoll where this impressive white hotel, complete with bell-tower, overlooks the meandering Guadaira river.

There is a particularly Spanish feel to the lofty public rooms; reception leads into a vaulted sitting-room of marble columns and ornamental Spanish vases. Its large French windows open on to a bougainvillaea-clad terrace where guests can sit and enjoy the view. Next door is a small cosy bar, serving *tapas* at red-and-white checked tables. The more formal dark green dining-room has fresh flowers on every table and sombre pictures of matadors on the walls. All service comes with a smile.

The bedrooms are in the main building and in a new extension which overlooks the swimming-pool and beds of roses and lilies. The rooms, decorated in light tones, vary in size but not quality. Some have balconies – a welcome extra in the heat of the Andalucian summer.

Nearby Seville (15 km) – cathedral and palaces.

Avenida de Portugal, 41500, Alcalá de Guadaira, Seville
Tel & fax (95) 5686400
Location amid pine trees, on hill overlooking town and river; with gardens and ample car parking
Meals breakfast, lunch, dinner
Prices rooms PP-PPPP; breakfast P; dinner PP
Rooms 26 doubles, one single, 3 family rooms; all with bath; all rooms have central heating, air-conditioning, phone, TV
Facilities dining-room, 2 sitting-rooms, bar/cafeteria, terrace; swimming-pool
Credit cards AE, DC, V
Children welcome
Disabled lift/elevator
Pets not accepted
Closed never
Manager Cristina Martinez

Seville

| Country guest-house, Aznalcazar |

Hacienda Dos Olivos

The name refers to the only two olive trees which had to be cut down to build this typical estate house a decade or so ago. A mixture of Andalucían, Moorish and modern, it is surrounded by a sea of olive groves which are farmed by the owners. Within easy reach of Seville, the property borders the vast Doñana National Park, and in the early evening you can see the resident eagles circling above.

Hacienda Dos Olivos is run very much as a private home. Meals are taken communaly, either in the candle-lit dining room, or, on fine evenings, beneath an olive tree in the gardens. The guest bedrooms, grouped around an inner patio, are simply furnished, with tiled floors and high sloping beamed ceilings. Only one has its own bathroom, the rest must share. It is possible to take the whole property for a single party, including La Casita, a little self-catering house within the courtyard which sleeps four.

The *raison d'être* of the Hacienda is its magnificent horses. Johanna Beattie-Batista is a renowned Classical dressage rider, and while staying here you can, if you wish, take lessons in the art.

Nearby Seville, 22 miles (35 km); Doñana National Park; Christopher Columbus sights on the Costa de la Luz.

Aznalcazar, Seville
Tel & fax (95) 575 05 62
Location outside Aznalcazar, 22 miles (35 km) SW of Seville; in own grounds with ample parking
Prices rooms P-PP; meals PP
Rooms 5 double and twin, one with bath, 4 sharing 2 bathrooms; all rooms have heating
Facilities sitting room, dining room, courtyard, terraces, gardens, swimming pool
Credit cards not accepted
Children welcome
Disabled rooms on ground floor
Pets not accepted
Closed never
Proprietor Johanna Beattie-Batista

Córdoba

Town house hotel, Córdoba

Hotel González

Hidden away in one of the narrow, white-washed streets in Córdoba's old Jewish quarter, just a stone's throw from the beautiful Mezquita, is this unusual little hotel, built in the remains of a 16thC Moorish palace and so far (we believe) undiscovered by other guidebooks. The only remaining 'remains' we could see were the rectangular stone doorway and one stone capital, but Joaquín and Manuel González have added plenty of Moorish touches, such as arabesque arches on the patio. They also run a souvenir shop adjoining the hotel, full of gaudy Moorish vases, but this does not affect (or reflect) the character of the hotel, which is run with a happy blend of informality and efficiency.

Our first impression was of a cool marble interior and a charming receptionist. The hall leads through the arches to a lovely patio, packed with pretty red and white dining-tables and copious flowers and greenery. Geraniums hang down from every possible ledge and balcony. There is also a modern bar where breakfast is served, and a rather dim sitting-room full of antique oil paintings. Upstairs, the bedrooms are simple and comfortable; most have small balconies looking over the patio.

Nearby Mezquita, Alcázar, old Jewish quarter.

Manríquez 3, 14003, Córdoba
Tel (957) 479819
Tel (957) 486187
Location in quiet street behind Mezquita (best found on foot); no private car parking – public car park
Meals breakfast, lunch, dinner
Prices rooms PP-PPP; breakfast P; meals PP
Rooms 15 double, 2 single, 3 family rooms, all with bath; all rooms have central heating, air-conditioning, phone, satellite TV, radio
Facilities dining-room/patio, sitting-room, cafeteria/bar, souvenir shop
Credit cards AE, MC, V
Children welcome
Disabled no special facilities
Pets not accepted
Closed restaurant only Nov
Proprietor Joaquín and Manuel González

Córdoba

Town hotel, Cordoba

Hotel Albucasis

We came upon this hotel, hidden in a quiet courtyard in the old Jewish quarter, completely by chance. It is only a couple of streets behind the Mezquita – escape the souvenir shops and bus-loads of tourists. The only indication of a hotel is a two-star sign outside an archway, leading into a stone-flagged courtyard. Ivy and apricot trees grow up the white, four-storey building inside the courtyard. You can sit out under the trees at iron tables and chairs, or relax in air-conditioned luxury on the other side of the French windows.

The interior is smart and new, tell-tale signs that the hotel was built only a few years ago. The main room doubles as a bar and breakfast area; it is a happy blend of old and new – modern furniture offset by old pistols and swords on the walls and an ancient wrought iron lamp in the middle of the room. Magazines and vases of fresh carnations add home-like touches.

The bedrooms are also smart and spotless, decorated in green and white. Most look on to the courtyard – those on the other side are smaller and have tiny bathrooms.

Nearby Mezquita, Alcázar, old Jewish quarter, archaeological museum.

Buen Pastor 11, 14003, Córdoba
Tel (957) 478625
Location in old Jewish quarter, 5 minutes walk from the Mezquita; car parking
Meals breakfast
Prices rooms PP; breakfast P
Rooms 9 double, 6 single, all with bath; all rooms have central heating, air-conditioning, phone
Facilities bar/sitting-room/ breakfast room, terrace
Credit cards MC, V
Children tolerated
Disabled access easy, lift/ elevator
Pets not accepted
Closed never
Proprietor Alfonso Salas

Córdoba

Converted monastery, Palma del Rio

Hospedería de San Francisco

This 15thC Franciscan monastery stands on a small square at the centre of a confusing one-way system. If you get lost, don't hesitate to ask for directions; everyone knows where the Hospedería is, as it becomes a focus of attention at fiesta time (the staff dress up as monks and run a bar behind the church).

The Moreno family converted the monastery into a hotel five years ago. The care they took is immediately obvious as you enter the main courtyard; tables are set up in the cloisters, where you can watch pigeons nesting in the bell-tower as you eat. The main dining-room is a high-ceilinged hall, dominated by a huge fireplace. All the sitting areas are comfortable, especially the tiled bar, with its beamed ceiling and old paintings. Some of the bedrooms were once monks' cells and are fairly small and basic, but what they lack in luxuries they make up for in character, with beautifully hand-painted basins and bed-covers woven by local nuns.

Chef Iñaki has an excellent reputation, and his caricature (round, moustached and wagging a long finger) adorns the constantly changing menu, which reflects his Basque origins.
Nearby Córdoba (55 km); Seville (90 km); churches and palaces in Écija and Carmona.

Avenida Pio X11, 14700,
Palma del Rio, Córdoba
Tel (957) 710732
Location on quiet square in heart of town; car parking
Meals breakfast, lunch, dinner
Prices rooms PP-PPPP; breakfast P; lunch PP, dinner PP
Rooms 14 double, one single, 2 family rooms, all with bath; all rooms have central heating, air-conditioning, phone, TV, safe

Facilities dining-room, sitting-room, bar, patio, cloisters
Credit cards AE, DC, MC, V
Children welcome
Disabled no special facilities
Pets accepted
Closed restaurant only, Sun dinner
Manager Iñaki Martínez

Jaén

Town mansion, Úbeda

PT Condestable Dávalos

Somewhat overshadowed by the lovely façade of the 16thC chapel next door to it, Úbeda's stately Parador stands on the Renaissance square of Vázquez de Molina. Its internal courtyard is delightful; sixteen slender pillars (on both floors) enclose a stone-flagged patio set with tables and chairs. Striking blue-and-white patterned tiles half cover the walls around the outside. A sweeping staircase leads to the glass-enclosed gallery, past suits of armour and a spectacular light inside a double-headed glass eagle. Some bedrooms are around the gallery, others look on to smaller leafy quads or the ornamental garden. There is more attention to detail here than in the average Parador – carved bed-heads, hand-painted mirrors and wooden writing desks.

Guests have the choice of two bars, the underground taberna or a bar-cum-sitting-room on the way to the gardens. Red-tiled floors with little picture inlays are found in all public rooms, including the attractive dining-room. It is a friendly and animated place, in which it is easy to relax – perhaps in the shade of giant ferns in the courtyard, or under pine trees in the garden. It seemed half the size of its 31 rooms, without being cramped – a great base for exploring this historic town.

Nearby Plaza, palaces, churches; Baeza (10 km); Jaén (55 km).

Plaza de Vázquez de Molina 1, 23400, Úbeda, Jaén
Tel (953) 750345
Location on square in historic part of town; follow signs; with car parking
Meals breakfast, lunch, dinner
Prices rooms PPPP; breakfast P; meals PP
Rooms 31 double, all with bath; all rooms have central heating, air-conditioning, phone, TV, minibar, hairdrier, radio
Facilities 2 dining-rooms, sitting-room, TV room, bar, cafeteria
Credit cards AE, DC, MC, V
Children welcome
Disabled access difficult
Pets not accepted, except guide dogs
Closed never
Manager José Muñoz Romera

Jaén

Aristocratic mansion, Úbeda

Palacio de la Rambla

There could be no more appropriate place to stay in the historic city of Úbeda than in this 16th century urban stately home, part of which has been opened to guests by the present Marquesa de la Rambla in order to help with the upkeep.

More a seignorial guest house than a hotel, the door of the Palacio de la Rambla is kept locked and you have to summon the caretaker via an intercom.

The central feature is the patio, dripping with ivy, which is one of Úbeda's Renaissance treasures. Around it are the four original rooms which are decorated with old engravings and family antiques. One has an old-fashioned blue bath on legs; the other has its own fireplace. The two other rooms on the ground floor have less character. We are told that a change of windows has eliminated the noise from those rooms overlooking the street. Another four rooms have been added upstairs at the front of the house.

Breakfast – 'whatever you want'– is brought to your room or served at one end of the salon. The grand piano at the other end holds the family photograph collection.

Nearby monuments of Úbeda; Baeza (11km); Cazorla Nature Reserve (55km).

Plaza del Marqués 1, 23400, Úbeda, Jaén
Tel (953) 750196
Location in the town centre; 4 garage places available
Meals breakfast (other meals for groups only by prior arrangement)
Prices bed and breakfast PPPP
Rooms 7 double, 1 suite, all with bath; all rooms have central heating, TV, minibar, telephone
Facilities sitting-room
Credit cards AE, V
Children accepted
Disabled access difficult
Pets not accepted
Closed 15 Jul to 15 Aug
Proprietor Elena Meneses de Orozco

Granada

Hotel América

Tucked away between the Alhambra and Granada's Parador (page 150), this delightful family-run hotel offers a perfect location at an affordable price. It is a small, friendly place, built around a vine-covered patio. In the summer months, the patio doubles as a dining-room – pretty tiled tables are set out, and you dine by the light of hanging lanterns to the sound of running water. The choice of dishes is limited, but everything is home-cooked, and if the smells coming from the kitchen when we visited are anything to go by, the food is delicious; it is also reasonably priced.

The bedrooms are small but comfortable and clean, and overlook either the patio or the gardens of the Alhambra. They are brightened up by colourful woven bedspreads and curtains. The sitting area next to the reception is crammed with pottery, ornaments, screens, sofas and rocking chairs – leaving hardly enough room to sit down. It is a small, busy hotel, and not the kind of place you would want to linger in all day. But with the Alhambra on your doorstep, there is more than enough to keep you busy.

Nearby Alhambra, Generalife and gardens, cathedral; Sierra Nevada (35 km), Costa del Sol (65 km).

Real de la Alhambra 53,
18009, Granada
Tel (958) 227471
Location inside walls of
Alhambra (follow road past
entrance); car parking
around square
Meals breakfast, lunch, dinner
Prices rooms PP-PPP, breakfast P; meals PP
Rooms 8 double, one family
room, all with bath; 4 single,
2 with bath, 2 with shower;
all rooms have central
heating, phone
Facilities dining-room,
sitting-room
Credit cards MC, V
Children accepted
Disabled one ground-floor
room
Pets not accepted
Closed 1 Dec to 28 Feb
Proprietor Rafael Garzón

Granada

Converted convent Parador, Granada

PT San Francisco

'Book at least three months in advance' was the advice that the management of this extremely popular Parador asked us to pass on; 'and more in high season', we would add. The attraction of this converted 14thC convent, set in the gardens of the famous Alhambra, is easy to see – especially when the day-trippers have disappeared – and the results are predictable.

Although the hotel is rather big and impersonal, it has some lovely touches – the chapel where Isabella of Spain was originally buried, now open to the sky, is used as a patio, and the adjoining courtyard full of plants and flowers is a place to sit and relax in lovely old rocking-chairs. Alcoves in the corridors and stairways are decorated with carved wooden figures of saints, and the stone-flagged floors are covered in bright Granadan rugs. The bedrooms are fairly standard, with large, tiled bathrooms; 32 of them have superb views over the Alhambra and the Generalife. Public rooms are comfortable, and there are seating areas on the terraces. The dining-room gets very busy – but any hotel near the Alhambra attracts crowds, and at least here you can sit and wait in glorious surroundings.

Nearby Alhambra, Generalife and gardens, cathedral; Sierra Nevada (35 km), Costa del Sol (65 km).

Real de la Alhambra, 18009, Granada
Tel (958) 221440
Fax (958) 222264
Location in Alhambra gardens (follow road past entrance); with garden and garage for 17 cars
Meals breakfast, lunch, dinner
Prices rooms PPPP; breakfast P; meals PP
Rooms 35 double, 3 single, all with bath; all rooms have central heating, air-conditioning, phone, TV, minibar, hairdrier
Facilities dining-room, sitting-room, bar
Credit cards AE, DC, MC, V
Children welcome
Disabled some ground-floor rooms
Pets not accepted
Closed never
Manager Juan Antonio Gianello

Granada

Villa Turística de Bubión

This is the first in a new concept of accommodation in Andalucia: a cluster of self-contained apartments built in the local style. The Villa Turística, run by a co-operative, recreates the architectural atmosphere of an Alpujarran village with its low-rise, flat topped houses, singular chimneys and shady alleyways. Compare it to the real thing in Bubión only a stone's throw down the hill.

There are three models of apartment, the largest having two bedrooms, two bathrooms and a sitting/dining room. All are decorated similarly, using local textiles and ceramics. Each has a fireplace – vital in the Alpujarras in winter – which room service will attend to. When we inspected, the authenticity of the rooms was only let down by the veneered kitchen cabinets, which we understand are being replaced.

The central block near the car-park houses reception, the dining-room/bar and a rather impersonal sitting-room upstairs – the sofas in front of reception are more inviting.

On weekdays the manager offers a reduced price to readers who present a copy of this guide.

Nearby walks in the Alpujarras; Bubión; Capileira (2km); the Veleta, by unsurfaced road to over 3,000 metres (25km).

Barrio Alto s/n, Bubión, Granada
Tel (958) 763111
Fax (958) 763136
Location above the village; car parking and garden
Meals breakfast, lunch, dinner
Prices rooms PPP; breakfast P; meals PP
Rooms 21 family , 18 double apartments, all with bath; all rooms have fireplace, TV, fridge, telephone
Facilities sitting-room, dining room, bar; mountain bikes
Credit cards AE, DC, MC, V
Children accepted
Disabled easy access
Pets accepted at extra charge
Closed never
Manager Victor Fernandez

Granada

Andalucian villa, Loja

La Bobadilla

Arches, tiles, white walls, iron grilles, fountains, plants, patios and balconies: La Bobadilla resembles a labyrinthine Andalucian village, set in its own 350-hectare grove of olives and evergreen oaks. More than one visitor has described it as the best hotel in Spain, indeed as one of the best in Europe and an inspection visit before this edition went to press confirmed that standards remain as high as ever.

There are 60 rooms: but what rooms. Most of them are enormous, with private garden or terrace. Every room is decorated with an abundance of marbles, silks and woodwork. The columns of the main hall are reminiscent of the mosque at Cordoba. There are concerts in the hotel chapel.

For outdoor entertainment, there is archery and clay-pigeon shooting; or you can ride, or drive a 4x4, through the olive groves. If you are still in need of variety, you can relax in the Turkish baths. The two restaurants are supplied by the hotel's own organic farm. The Finca is locally renowned; El Cortijo is the more intimate. There is not a corner, patio or corridor which does not boast some atmospheric detail: splashes of greenery, the gurgles of water seem to greet you at every turn.

Nearby Archidona (18km); Antequera (35 km); Granada (70 km).

Finca La Bobadilla, 18300, Loja, Granada
Tel (958) 321861
Location 3 km on the C334 from Salinas to Iznajar; car parking
Meals breakfast, lunch, dinner
Prices rooms PPPP, breakfast PP; meals PPP
Rooms 49 double (29 with sitting room), 2 single, 9 suites, all with bath; all rooms have air- conditioning, phone, minibar, TV (satellite)
Facilities 2 restaurants, bar, meeting room; 2 swimming-pools, terrace, sauna, Turkish baths, massage; tennis-court, mountain bikes; shops, chapel, beauty salon, hair-dressers **Credit cards** AE, DC, MC, V **Children** accepted
Disabled 2 rooms with special facilities **Pets** only in rooms
Closed never
Manager Miguel del Valle

Almería

San José

Spain's extreme south-east corner has escaped the excesses of package holiday tourism and this hotel is ideally located to enjoy some of the last unspoilt beaches on the Mediterranean coast.

The house, reminiscent of a Swiss chalet, was formerly a warehouse for *esparto* – a grass traditionally used to make shoes and baskets.

Large semi-circular windows illuminate the sitting-room and allow you to look down on the beach or gaze out to sea. The whole place is full of entertaining details. A parrot in a large cage on a pedestal is kept covered up to stop it talking. Beyond the dining-room an intimate salon has a rustic cot, an old barber's chair and a collection of sea urchins and shells.

The best bedrooms are the two on the second floor facing the sea. All the rooms have character with their antique tiled floors and colonial ceiling fans. But the enormous bathrooms are marred by their antiquated plumbing and fittings – which may convince you that the hotel is overpriced.

Tourists fill San José in the summer months. In the winter the place is dead, or peaceful, as you prefer, but the climate is still warm and sunny.

Nearby Cabo de Gata nature reserve; Almeria (40km).

Correo s/n, 04118, San José
Almería
Tel (950) 380116
Location on the beach in San José; garden and car parking
Meals breakfast, lunch, dinner
Prices rooms PPP-PPPP; breakfast P; meals PP
Rooms 8 double with bath; all rooms have ceiling fan, safe, TV
Facilities dining-room, bar, meeting rooms; terrace, private beach, solarium, sitting-room
Credit cards MC, V
Children accepted
Disabled access difficult
Pets not accepted
Closed Oct to Mar
Manager Eduardo G. Zárate

Almeria

Balneario de Sierra Alhamilla

Nothing could be more relaxing after a day in the car than to slip into this spa hotel's heated swimming-pool with its underwater massage jets.

Inside the hotel you can shut yourself away from the bleak surroundings of arid mountains and relax in modest comfort. Peace reigns day and night: the only sound in the patio is the trickle of a fountain.

The original building was raised in 1777 by the Bishop of Almeria on the site of Roman baths. A few years ago the ruins were faithfully reconstructed by the present owner, the polite and quietly-spoken Isidro Pérez.

The dining-room is in a barrel-vaulted chamber decorated with patterned tiles and Mudejar plasterwork. The food is well-intentioned and daintily presented on octagonal plates but not of outstanding quality. Breakfast is served under the brick dome of the Bishop's former chapel, looked down upon by an altarpiece.

The bedrooms are old-fashioned with double doors and arched ceilings. Some of the bathrooms suffer from a few niggling, though unimportant, defects.

Nearby Las Millares neolithic necropolis (20km); Mini-Hollywood film sets (22km); solar power station (35km).

04259, Pechina, Almeria
Tel (950) 317413
Fax (950) 160257
Location turn off N 340 for Chuche; hotel is signposted from Pechina; car parking
Meals breakfast, lunch, dinner
Prices rooms PP-PPP; breakfast P; meals PP
Rooms 16 double, 8 suites, all with bath; all rooms have central heating, TV, telephone

Facilities sitting-room, dining- room, breakfast room, spa facilities, heated swiming-pool
Credit cards AE, MC, V
Children accepted
Disabled easy access
Pets not accepted
Closed never
Proprietor Isidro Pérez

Cádiz

Casa del Corregidor

A white mansion on the edge of a formidable cliff. Flower-patterned tiles border the white walls along the corridors; ceramic pictures tell the stories of bullfights; and potted plants fill the pebbled internal courtyard. Eight of the rooms enjoy views over the patchwork of fields and orchards far below. Some of the others look onto the main square of Arcos and the lovely 16thC church of Santa María.

Both the bar and dining-room have French windows opening on to large sunny cliff-top terraces. Order the *menu degustación* to sample a range of regional specialities.

Nearby Jerez (30 km); Cádiz (63km); Grazalema (50 km).

Plaza de España, 11630, Arcos de la Frontera, Cádiz
Tel (956) 700500
Fax (956) 701116
Location on main square, next to Santa Maria (follow Parador signs); with car parking in square
Meals breakfast, lunch, dinner
Prices rooms PPP-PPPP; breakfast P; meals PP
Rooms 20 double, 4 single, all with bath; all rooms have central heating, air-conditioning, phone, TV, minibar, radio
Facilities dining-room, 2 sitting-rooms, bar, 2 terraces
Credit cards AE, DC, MC, V
Children accepted
Disabled lift/elevator
Pets not accepted
Closed never
Manager Máximo Pérez

Paradores in Andalucía

The two Paradores in Huelva are both modern. The 53-room PT Costa de la Luz at Ayamonte, on the borders of Portugal, is a sprawling white building high above the city, with magnificent views (Tel (955) 320700). The 43-room PT Cristóbal Colón is on the coast, just beyond Mazágon; a footpath goes down to a sandy beach (Tel (955) 376000). Cádiz has a large modern Parador, a six-storey white complex called the Atlántico, on the south side of the isthmus. Ask for a room with a sea view (Tel (956) 226905).

The Costa del Sol has three Paradores. Two are close to Málaga – as well as the PT de Gibralfaro (see page 168) there is the self-explanatory Golf, a little way west of the town (Tel (952) 381255). The third is at Nerja: large and modern but attractive, with well-furnished rooms and an elevator down to the beach (Tel (952) 520050). North-east of Almería is PT Reyes Católicos at Mojácar (Tel (950) 478250), which feels more intimate than its 98 rooms would suggest.

Inland, the Paradores at Antequera, Arcos de la Frontera, Carmona, Granada, Jaén and Úbeda have detailed entries. The modern 83-room PT de la Arruzafa at Córdoba is 3 km from the middle of the city (Tel (957) 275900). The dismal PT de Bailén has little to recommend it apart from its pool (Tel (953) 670100). Much more appealing is the PT El Adelantado at Cazorla – (Tel (953) 721075).

Cádiz

Converted convent, Arcos de la Frontera

El Convento

In 1990 our inspectors counted this hotel, in part of a convent in the old town of Arcos, as one of their favourites in Andalucia. Readers have subsequently confirmed this judgement – although one felt the place to be pretentious and over-hyped. Extensive changes are being made this year to provide more spacious public areas and a café, so we welcome further reports.

Certainly the owners, José Antonio Roldán and his wife María Moreno, could not be more welcoming; but neither does Sr Roldán miss an opportunity to promote his enterprise. The corridor walls are papered with press cuttings.

The number of rooms has increased to fourteen; they are homely, and sometimes decorated with ingenuous taste. Each year one of them is formally dedicated to a 'famous' son of Arcos. Five of the rooms have terraces and most enjoy panoramic views to rival those of the nearby Parador. Breakfast is served in the convent's former sacristy – a white arched chamber – and there is bar service during the day. For other meals you have to stroll round to the Roldán's garlanded restaurant, one minute's walk away, in the attractive 16th century Valdespino palace. Specialities include Arcos garlic soup and home-made desserts.

Nearby churches of Santa María and San Pedro; Jerez (30 km).

Calle Maldonado 2, 11630, Arcos de la Frontera, Cádiz
Tel & fax (956) 702333
Location on a tiny back street, past church and Parador; car parking in main square
Meals breakfast, lunch, dinner
Prices rooms P-PP; breakfast P; meals PP
Rooms 5 double, 3 single, all with bath; all rooms have central heating, phone, TV
Facilities 2 dining-rooms, bar, 2 terraces
Credit cards AE, MC, V
Children welcome
Disabled access difficult
Pets not accepted
Closed never
Proprietor María Moreno

Cádiz

Hotel Los Olivos

The receptionist at the Olivos told us (in good English) that the hotel is usually full; it is easy to see why. It is an attractive place, even from the outside – built in typical Arcos style with white-washed walls, yellow tiled roofs and iron grills over the windows, and equipped with pots of geraniums on arched balconies. But it is the interior that really captivates.

The rooms are built around an internal courtyard; café-style tables and chairs are set out in the middle, under a palm tree. The breakfast room is decorated in the same dark green furniture and doubles up as a bar; it looks on to a tiny patio containing an old stone well. Behind the glass arches surrounding the courtyard is a cosy alcove with wicker sofas and armchairs, and bowls of fresh flowers.

The bedrooms are light and airy – comfortable, but not cluttered with furniture. All have different cane bedsteads, pale covers and curtains, and mats covering stone-tiled floors. The two front bedrooms have balconies with sweeping views over the plains and the nearby olive-groves from which the hotel takes its name.

Nearby churches of Santa María and San Pedro, castle; Jerez, Cádiz, Ronda within driving distance.

San Miguel 2, 11630, Arcos de la Frontera, Cádiz
Tel (956) 700811
Fax (956) 702018
Location on road up to Parador, overlooking Guadalete plains; car parking on street
Meals breakfast
Prices rooms P-PP; breakfast P
Rooms 18 double, 2 single; all with bath; all rooms have central heating, air-conditioning, phone, TV, minibar, radio
Facilities sitting-rooms, TV room, bar/breakfast room
Credit cards AE, MC, V
Children welcome
Disabled lift/elevator
Pets not accepted
Closed never
Proprietor Raquel Roldán

Cádiz

Andalucian villa, Arcos de la Frontera

Cortijo Faín

This landowner's residence, or cortijo, stands in the middle of a vast olive grove not far from one of the most spectacular of the White Towns. The silence is only broken by the odd tractor ploughing between the trees.

The house and outbuildings enclose a pretty courtyard with a well and drinking trough in the middle. Most of the rooms are upstairs in the main house. They are of varying shapes and sizes but all warmly furnished with antiques, iron or brass bedsteads, crocheted bedspreads, books and flowers. On the first-floor landing is a small household chapel.

Equally inviting are the rustically decorated public rooms littered with oil paintings and more antiques. The cafeteria is in the old stables. From the sitting-room, a door leads into the library: an even more relaxing room lined with 7,000 leather-bound volumes. The dining room has a glass-enclosed porch opening on to the garden.

From the back of the house a path leads across the lawn between the olive trees to a large, curving swimming-pool crossed by a hump-backed bridge.

Nearby Arcos de la Frontera (3km); Grazalema (53km). Carretera de Algar, Km 3,

11630, Arcos de la Frontera Cádiz.
Tel (956) 701167
Fax (956) 231396
Location from Arcos take the road towards El Algar and turn off left (signposted) after 3 km; garden and car parking
Meals breakfast, lunch, dinner
Prices rooms PP-PPPP; breakfast P; meals PP
Rooms 3 double, 1 single, 4 suites, one apartment, all with bath; all rooms have air conditioning, radiator
Facilities dining-room, sitting-room, bar, swimming-pool
Credit cards AE, MC, V
Children welcome
Disabled 3 ground floor rooms
Pets accepted
Closed never
Proprietor José Luis Jiminez Rodriguez

Cádiz

Converted convent, Vejer de la Frontera

Convento de San Francisco

Vejer is a delightful medieval town crowning a solitary hill near the coast. In the old part of town, the Felipe brothers have lovingly converted a 17thC convent into an unusual hotel; a set of photographs in the echoing *taberna* tell the story of the renovations. Many of the remains have been preserved – a Roman mosaic in the hall, a cabinet of medieval pottery on the stairs, the old choir stalls and frescos in the sitting-room. The bedrooms still have their original stone arches visible in the walls and the furniture has been designed in harmony – arched bedheads, stripped pine desks, wooden shutters. The result is effective – the simplicity of a nun's cell with the facilities of a modern hotel.

The refectory still serves as a dining-room, still with wooden benches and tables lining the walls. Bright modern cushions and abstract modern paintings add a splash of colour. Our inspector's meal, the *menu del dia*, was excellent, piping hot and served by cheerful staff. Outside the dining-room is an obscure metal sculpture, two floors high. The centre-piece of the Convento is the 'choir hall' – a great place to sit when the sun filters through the windows in the early morning.

Nearby Castle, churches, Jewish Quarter.

La Plazuela, 11150, Vejer de la Frontera, Cádiz
Tel (956) 451001
Location on small square in old part of town, round corner from main street on cliff edge; car parking on main street
Meals breakfast, lunch, dinner
Prices rooms PP-PPP; breakfast P; menu PP
Rooms 18 double, 5 single, one family room; all with bath; all rooms have electric heating, phone, TV
Facilities dining-room, sitting-room, cafeteria, bar
Credit cards DC, MC, V
Children welcome
Disabled lift/elevator
Pets not accepted
Closed never
Manager Jesús Felipe Gallego

Cádiz

Converted convent, La Almoraima

Casa Convento

Opposite a large factory on the main road to Jimena, a small sign points up a wooded drive to the Casa Convento. Following the road, you pass from scrubby trees dotted with nesting boxes to beautiful landscaped gardens, and end up in front of the yellow and white façade of a 17thC convent. Tall palm trees shade the arched windows and elegant pillars along the front of the building. The place is serene – it comes as quite a surprise to discover that until recently it was a hunting lodge (witness the mounted hunting trophies in the public rooms).

Despite its grandiose appearance, the hotel is surprisingly informal and relaxed; the public rooms are obviously used, not just admired. The 'bar' consists of a trolley of spirits, the 'games room' a billiard table, the 'music room' a mini grand piano, and the 'library' a couple of ancient book shelves. The rooms upstairs are reminiscent of an English country house – with tapestries on the sitting-room walls and chandeliers over the long dining-room table. Bedrooms are comfortable, overlooking either the gardens or the central courtyard. The chapel and the old bell-towers are the only reminders that this was once a convent.

Nearby Castellar de la Frontera; Algeciras (25 km).

La Almoraima, 11350, Castellar de la Frontera, Cádiz
Tel (956) 693002
Location in wooded grounds, 12 km north of Algeciras on N340; with gardens and car parking
Meals breakfast, lunch, dinner
Prices rooms PP-PPPP; breakfast P; meals PP
Rooms 7 double, 4 single; all with bath; all rooms have central heating, phone; most rooms have fires, some rooms have TV
Facilities dining room, sitting-room, games room; swimming-pool, tennis court, mini-golf, horse riding
Credit cards AE, DC, MC, V
Children not accepted
Disabled access difficult
Pets accepted in bedrooms
Closed never
Manager Juan Montoya

Cádiz

Town house, Sanlúcar de Barrameda

Posada de Palacio

Antonio and Renata Navarrete set up this pension in 1986, when they moved from Switzerland. It is a typical Andalucian town house, near the Bombadilla sherry bodegas in the old part of the town. If you get lost, follow your nose; an overpowering smell of Sanlúcar's famous manzanilla lingers around the warehouses.

The guest-house is built around a courtyard of original stone floor-tiles. Most of the bedrooms are in this part of the building, including two ground-floor suites. All the rooms are unconventional, adding to their charm. Some could benefit from refurbishment, but all are clean and comfortable, and those we saw were very spacious – we had a cavernous bathroom, even bigger than our bedroom. We ate a superb home-made breakfast in our room overlooking the tiny garden.

The public rooms are full of interesting objects that the couple have collected over the years; an old grinding wheel hangs next to modern film posters in the bar, miniature pictures decorate the walls, and fresh flowers abound. You are constantly reminded that this is a home as well as a hotel. Tables are set outside under the wistaria, and up ivy-covered steps, four new rooms look on to a large stone sun-terrace.

Nearby Castle, palace, sherry bodegas, beach.

Calle Caballeros 11, 11540, Sanlúcar de Barrameda, Cádiz
Tel (956) 364840
Fax (956) 365060
Location near castle and palace, in old part of town; car parking on street
Meals breakfast, dinner
Prices rooms PP; breakfast P; dinner PP
Rooms 8 double, 4 with bath, 4 with shower, 2 single with bath, 3 suites, with bath; all rooms have phone
Facilities sitting-room, TV room, bar/breakfast room, terrace, dining-room
Credit cards MC, V
Children welcome
Disabled ground-floor rooms
Pets accepted
Closed Jan and Feb
Proprietor Antonio and Renata Navarrete

Cádiz

Tartaneros

Most of the ground floor of the Tartaneros is given over to an elegant *art nouveau* cafeteria spreading through various drawing rooms, rich in ornamental period detail.

The hotel, reached through a door beside the bar, is less distinguished but also furnished with eclectic taste. The large open-plan sitting-room is littered with maritime memorabilia and other curios including a bullfighter's suit of lights.

The bedrooms are dotted with antique furniture. Those on the ground floor are in the vaults of old wine cellar. The upstairs rooms are bigger.

Nearby palace, sherry bodegas; Jerez de la Frontera (22km).

Calle Tartaneros 8, 11540, Sanlúcar de Barrameda, Cádiz
Tel (956) 362044
Fax (956) 360045
Location in the city centre; no garden or car parking
Meals breakfast
Prices rooms PP; breakfast P
Rooms 18 double, 4 single, all with bath; all rooms have central heating, air-conditioning, TV, minibar, telephone, safe
Facilities cafeteria, sitting-room
Credit cards AE, DC, MC, V
Children accepted
Disabled easy access to ground floor rooms
Pets small ones only
Closed never
Proprietor Enrique Pérez

Hotel Grazalema

Grazalema's only hotel is on the edge of the town. The spectacular views from the hotel's terraces – mile upon mile of olive and pine groves, meadows of flowers and towering mountains (all part of a nature reserve) – never fail to bring whoops of joy from newly arrived visitors.

The interior is mainly open-plan, with a reception area, bar and sitting-room on one level and a pretty white dining-room on a lower level. Striped hand-woven rugs and curtains, made on old wooden looms in the village, brighten up the white walls. Arched French windows open on to the lawns and swimming-pool area.

Nearby Zahara de la Sierra (23km); Ronda (31km).

Carretera Comarcal 334, 11610, Grazalema, Cádiz
Tel (956) 141162
Location on hill on edge of village; with garden and car parking
Meals breakfast, lunch, dinner
Prices rooms PP; breakfast P; meals PP
Rooms 24 double, all with bath; all rooms have central heating, phone
Facilities dining-room, sitting-room, TV room, terrace; swimming-pool
Credit cards V
Children accepted
Disabled no special facilities
Pets not accepted
Closed never
Manager Rodrigo Valle Naranjo

Cádiz

Hotels on the Costa del Sol

'Charming' and 'small' are not the first adjectives that spring to mind when considering hotels along the Costa del Sol. It has taken some searching to find such places along this 200 km holiday playground, and many of the hotels we describe in detail are not actually on the coast but behind it, hidden away in the mountains. Anyone who wants to be on the coast itself might consider some of the hotels listed below. A word of warning though: most of them get booked up in high season, so plan well in advance.

Tarifa – an unspoilt fishing village 22 km south-west of Algeciras – is not technically part of the Costa del Sol, but the 28-room Hurricane (Tel (956) 684919), is a paradise for wind-surfers and outdoor types.

The pick of Gibraltar's hotels is the Rock (Tel (350) 73000), a large, rather old-fashioned establishment serving traditional British food.

Just outside San Pedro de Alcántara is the Cortijo de los Caballos (Tel (952) 886767), a complex of 12 bungalow apartments around a swimming-pool and one of the few places in Spain not to accept children.

The true heart of the Costa del Sol is Marbella, the most up-market of the resorts. One of the more stylish places to stay here is the Marbella Club (Tel (952) 771300) which is set in luxuriant gardens.

Further round the coast, after the package holiday resorts of Fuengirola and Torremolinos, comes Málaga. More than an airport it is a sprawling city which is best avoided in high season. If you have to stay here, the Palacio – luxurious, with a roof-top pool (Tel (952) 215185) – and Casa Curro (Tel (952) 227200) – central, comfortable – are good alternatives to the Parador. Most hotels run a bus service to the airport.

East of Málaga the coast is less built up. The famous view from the Balcón de Europa, in Nerja, is definitely worth stopping for and you could do worse than stay in Cala Bella in the heart of town, a friendly, family run hotel with a superb terrace where guests dine in summer (Tel (952) 520700).

The 47-room Los Fenicios (Tel (958) 640025), in the small resort of La Herradura stands out from the blocks around it because of its original architecture and its unusual brass and glass lift.

The holiday strip terminates in the dry province of Almeria. In the city of the same name, the Torreluz IV (Tel (951) 234799) is brashly modern but distinguished by white leather sofas, a spiral staircase and a roof-top swimming pool.

Hotel Prices
As we explain in the introduction, many hotels did not know their future prices when we were preparing this edition. It is always wise to check when making a booking or checking in. Note that most hotels quote their rates excluding VAT (IVA in Spanish – usually 6%).

Málaga

Hostal Avalon

Since our last edition, this neat, modern *hostal* which used to be run by a Swedish couple, has changed hands and now has English owners, so we look forward to receiving reports on any differences in approach.

You eat on the covered terrace above the garden or at one end of the open-plan sitting/dining area. At the other end of this airy room are comfortable sofas next to a bookshelf of well-thumbed novels, and opposite is a smart modern bar. Public space may be limited when the hotel is full, but there is always the garden or the large, red-brick roof terrace (if you are feeling too lazy to cross the road to the beach).

All but one of the bedrooms have balconies with sea views; they are decorated in pastel shades, and are clean and comfortable.

This is the kind of place you can treat like home; there is even a well-equipped kitchen for guests staying more than a week. The only reservation we have is that the *hostal* is built above the busy coast road. But the Avalon's fabulous views of the sea and mountains more than make up for the dull murmur of traffic.

Nearby beach; Nerja (2 km), Málaga (47 km).

Punta Lara, 29780, Nerja, Málaga
Tel (952) 520698
Location on main road from Nerja to Málaga, 2 km from town; with garden and shaded car parking in drive
Meals breakfast, lunch, dinner
Prices rooms P-PP; breakfast P; lunch PP, dinner PP
Rooms 8 double, 5 with shower, 3 with bath; extra beds available; all rooms have electric heaters
Facilities dining-room/ sitting-room/bar, 2 terraces
Credit cards accepted
Children welcome; but not safe for small children
Disabled one ground-floor room
Pets welcome
Closed never
Proprietor Richard Keniry and Paul Mathews

Málaga

Town house hotel, Torremolinos

Hotel Miami

Somewhere in the ocean of concrete formed by the merger of Málaga and Torremolinos, a small sign directs you off the main coast road to the Miami. It is set in its own rounded driveway and is completely walled off from its surroundings – it feels just like an island. The house was built by Picasso's cousin as a holiday villa and has made an unusual hotel, set around a lagoon-like swimming pool. Palms and banana trees overshadow the pool and give it an exotic, tropical feel – you could be in the Caribbean rather than in the heart of Torremolinos, only yards away from a crowded beach and busy sea-front.

Some of the bedrooms are in need of attention; ours was worn and dusty, but adequate. Most have balconies, and all are cool and airy. One of the key features of the hotel is the grotto-like sitting-room, with its mixture of square and round windows peeping out of pebble-dashed walls and its curious fireplace of piled stones. It is full of interesting objects – animal-skin seats, copper pots, pilot lanterns.

There is no restaurant, but the Miami does serve probably the only 'Spanish' breakfast in Torremolinos – on the terrace above the pool.

Nearby beach; Málaga (15 km), Marbella (45 km).

Calle Aladino 14, 29620, Torremolinos, Málaga
Tel (952) 385255
Location on quiet side-street, 50 m from beach; signed from main road through Torremolinos; with garden and ample car parking in drive
Meals breakfast
Prices rooms P-PP; breakfast P
Rooms 23 double, 3 single, all with bath; all rooms have central heating, phone, TV, safe
Facilities sitting-room, bar/patio, swimming-pool
Credit cards not accepted
Children accepted; play area
Disabled 6 ground-floor rooms
Pets accepted
Closed never
Manager Mercedes Gómez

Málaga

Modern Parador, Antequera

PT de Antequera

Although it is large and modern, this was one of our favourite Paradors, with exceptionally welcoming and helpful staff (so often the Parador weakness). It is set on a hill, overlooking plains and mountains and the pretty white town of Antequera. The two wings of the white building look on to a magnificent swimming-pool, surrounded by lawns and shady trees. Most bedrooms face this way, and have either direct access to the gardens or balconies overlooking them. The rooms are large, cool and comfortable, and have the most powerful showers in Spain.

The dining-room and split-level sitting-room are reminiscent of an Alpine chalet – add snow to the craggy mountain tops seen through the large windows, and you could be in Switzerland. The food, however, is definitely Spanish – delicious shellfish, local trout, paella, almond tarts. All the public rooms are large and formal; sofas, rocking-chairs and card tables are set out as if they were on display, not in use. Yet the atmosphere in the rest of the Parador is relaxed and informal (although one visitor's peace was marred by the presence of a conference group). An excellent base for exploring the surrounding countryside and the fascinating prehistoric monuments in the town.

Nearby Roman remains, castle; Costa del Sol (50 km).

Paseo García del Olmo,
29200, Antequera, Málaga
Tel (952) 840901
Location on hill on edge of town; with gardens and car parking
Meals breakfast, lunch, dinner
Prices rooms PP-PPP, breakfast P; meals PP
Rooms 55 double, all with bath; all rooms have central heating, air-conditioning, phone, TV, minibar

Facilities dining-room, 2 sitting-rooms, bar; swimming-pool
Credit cards AE, DC, MC, V
Children welcome
Disabled ground-floor rooms
Pets not accepted
Closed never
Manager Manuel Martínez

Málaga

Hilltop Parador, Málaga

PT de Málaga-Gibralfaro

If you have time to spare in Málaga, spend it at this Parador, set in the peaceful gardens of the Gibralfaro on a hilltop above the city. It is the setting and the spectacular views, rather than the hotel itself, that make it an exceptional place to stay in this drab concrete port. This Parador is often thronged with people who come up here to escape the heat and hassle, and to enjoy the views of the port and Costa del Sol while they dine on the terraces.

The approach road winds through pine and eucalyptus trees, ending up at an stone-arcaded building, just below the remains of the Phoenician/Moorish castle. Throughly renovated and refurbished in 1995, while tripling the number of its bedrooms, the Parador de Málaga-Gibralfaro has all the usual facilities – spacious bedrooms with large balconies, a busy bar serving excellent snacks, and an attractive dining-room with tables outside under the arches, and the addition of a new outdoor swimming-pool.

Dining up here, with the sea shimmering below you and Gibraltar just visible in the distance, it is hard to believe that you are in the heart of Málaga.

Nearby gardens of Gibralfaro, Alcazaba; Costa del Sol.

Monte de Gibralfaro, 29016, Málaga
Tel (952) 221902
Fax (952) 221904
Location on hill above city, next to castle; with gardens and shaded car parking
Meals breakfast, lunch, dinner
Prices rooms PPPP; breakfast P; meals PP
Rooms 38 double, all with bath; all rooms have central heating, air-conditioning, phone, TV, minibar
Facilities dining-room, sitting-room/bar, terrace, swimming-pool
Credit cards AE, DC, MC, V
Children welcome
Disabled 1 specially equipped room
Pets not accepted
Closed never
Manager Juan Carlos García Alonso

Málaga

Old water-mill, Benaoján

Molino del Santo

A short drive (or train-ride) from Ronda is the sleepy village of Benaoján, perched on a herb-scented mountainside, surrounded by olive and almond groves. Its water-mill, beside the bubbling stream below the village, was converted into a hotel in 1987 by a young English couple, Andy Chapell and Pauline Elkin, who fled the rat-race in favour of this idyllic spot. We could see why as soon as we arrived, on a timeless Sunday morning when the guests were eating a leisurely buffet breakfast under the willow trees on the stone terrace. Dinner is also served out here in the summer (a delicious-sounding set menu with plenty of choice and vegetarian options). To the amusement of the locals, guests also get a real English tea with home-made cakes.

Inside, the rooms are comfortable and home-like; the sitting-area still has some of its original trappings – such as the old grinding stones. The bedrooms vary in size (some take extra beds) and are simply furnished, with bright locally made rugs. Twelve have small terraces overlooking a beautiful swimming-pool, shaded by willow, fig and quince trees.

Andy and Pauline rent out mountain bikes for exploring, and provide information for excursions to all the local sights.
Nearby cave of La Pileta – paleolithic art; white towns.

Bda Estación, 29370, Benaoján, Málaga
Tel (952) 167151
Fax (952) 167327
E-mail molino@logiccontrol.es
Location near railway station; with gardens, car parking
Meals breakfast, lunch, tea, dinner
Prices rooms PP-PPP; breakfast P; meals PP *á la carte*; children's meals available
Rooms 14 double, 10 with bath, 2 family rooms with shower; all rooms have central heating, tea and coffee facilities
Facilities dining-room, bar, terrace; solar hea3ted pool
Credit cards AE, DC, MC, V
Children welcome
Disabled access difficult
Pets not accepted
Closed 10 Dec to end Feb
Proprietor Andy Chapell and Pauline Elkin

Málaga

Hunting lodge, Ojén

Refugio de Juanar

Parador signs still point the way from Ojén to the Refugio in the wild foothills of the Sierra Blanca, although it ceased to be a Parador several years ago. Now run (at least as efficiently as it ever was) by the local authorities, it has become a popular mountain retreat from the pressure of the Costa del Sol – for locals and tourists alike.

It was built as a hunting lodge at the turn of the century and still retains its 'hunting' atmosphere. The sitting-room is an informal jumble of leather sofas around a log fire – deer antlers and zebra skin hang among old English hunting scenes on the walls. Photographs in the bar show wildlife from around the Refugio – ibex and peacocks on the lawns, birds of prey in action. The bedrooms are comfortably rustic and smell of woodsmoke. The restaurant continues on the hunting theme, specializing in game casseroles and local produce. It opens out on to a terrace overlooking pine trees.

Apart from the neat swimming-pool and tennis court, the grounds are wonderfully wild – the perfect place for children of an appropriate age to go exploring. No one with a taste for the outdoors is likely to get bored here.

Nearby National Reserve; Ojén (10 km); Marbella (20 km).

Sierra Blanca, 29610, Ojén, Málaga
Tel (952) 881000
Location in mountains, 10 km from Ojen; follow signs to Refugio; with grounds and car parking in drive
Meals breakfast, lunch, dinner
Prices rooms PP-PPP; breakfast P; meals PP
Rooms 18 double, one single, 2 family rooms, 2 suites; all with bath; all rooms have central heating, phone, minibar, TV, safe
Facilities dining-room, sitting-room, TV room, bar; swimming-pool, tennis court, table tennis
Credit cards AE, DC, MC, V
Children accepted
Disabled some ground-floor rooms **Pets** not accepted
Closed never
Manager José Gómez Avila

Málaga

Country inn, Alhaurín el Grande

Finca La Mota

Behind a high white wall in the lush countryside outside the village of Alhaurín lies this three-hundred-year-old farmhouse, now run as a friendly country inn by a British/American combination, Jean and Arun Narang. The hotel's six-acre lawns and shady trees surround a swimming-pool, but for those wanting sand and sea, the Costa del Sol is only a short drive away through the mountains. Most guests prefer the peace of the Andalucian countryside, and enjoy the beautiful walks or rides (on the family ponies) in the surrounding hills.

The rooms at Finca La Mota are pleasantly rustic, with open fires for cold winter days and a mixture of English and Andalucian antiques, collected by the Narangs over the years. Some have four-poster beds. One of our readers who visited recently, however, was disappointed by the quality of the room that he was offered.

The Narangs' restaurant is very popular, offering interesting dishes that are far from the Spanish norm (including Indian and Malaysian curries) and plenty of fresh vegetables from the garden. They are happy to cook guests' special requests and have a big barbecue every weekend.

Nearby Coín (10 km); Málaga (25 km).

Partido Urique, 29100,
Alhaurín El Grande, Málaga
Tel (952) 490901
Location in agricultural
countryside about 2 km SW
on mijas road out of Alhaurin;
with garden and car parking
Meals breakfast, lunch, dinner
Prices rooms PP with
English breakfast; meals PP
Rooms 9 double, 5 with bath;
2 family room with bath;
all rooms have tea/coffee kit
and electric heaters; all rooms
have TV
Facilities dining-room,
sitting-room, bar, terrace;
swimming-pool, tennis court,
mini-golf, riding
Credit cards AE, DC, MC, V
Children welcome
Disabled 4 ground-floor rooms
Pets accepted
Closed never
Proprietors Arun and Jean
Narang

Málaga

Converted farmhouse, Carretera de Monda

Santa Fe

A newcomer to guide, this delightful rural retreat was first recommended to us by a correspondent who discovered it by accident and was so 'delighted by the standard of accomodation, the cuisine and the wonderful location' that she and her husband immediately booked a return visit.

Set high up overlooking the Guadalhorce valley, Santa Fe is a typical Andalucían farmhouse which has been sympathetically restored by its warm and welcoming Dutch owners. Rooms are light and airy, decorated in keeping with the rustic character of the house with terracotta floors and beamed ceilings. The food is a highlight, with imaginative menus using local produce, including a vegetarian selection. 'Don't miss the creamed spinach and langoustine' says our reporter. In summer months meals can be taken outside on the terrace, under the shade of an old olive tree, and in winter in the attractive dining-room. From the terraces which surround the hotel, the lovely gardens, and the inviting swimming pool there are marvellous views in almost every direction. The surrounding countryside, with its groves of orange and lemon, is perfect for walking or riding.

Nearby Monda, 3 miles (5 km); Marbella and the Costa del Sol, 12 miles (20 km).

Carretera de Monda 3 km, Apartado 147, 29100 Coín, Málaga
Tel (95) 245 2916
Fax (95) 245 3843
Location off the C337 Monda to Coín road; in gardens with ample parking
Meals breakfast, lunch, dinner
Prices rooms PP; meals PP
Rooms 3 double with bath, 2 double with shared bath
Facilities sitting room, bar, dining room, terraces, garden, swimming pool
Credit cards DC, MC, V,
Children welcome
Disabled access difficult
Pets accepted
Closed 2 weeks Nov, 2 weeks Jan
Proprietors Arjan and Warden van de Vrande

Mallorca

Hotels on the Balearic Islands

The *Islas Báleares* consist of four islands. Largest and most well-known is Mallorca, a popular holiday destination comprising beautiful sandy beaches in the south, and towering mountains, sheer cliffs and rocky coves in the north. One of the island's smartest hotels is on its northernmost point, the Cap de Formentor – the luxurious 130-room Formentor (Tel (971) 865300), splendidly set amidst pine trees on the edge of a beach. It has excellent facilities, especially for children, and comfortable rooms with perfect views of sea and peaks. Deia, close to the rugged north-west coast, has two smart hotels of note; La Residencia (page 173) and the Es Molí, which is stunningly situated on the edge of the cliff. The rooms have recently been redecorated and the gardens are luxurious, 'a dazzling array of trailing flowers, laden fruit trees and immaculate lawns, lovingly tended by an army of gardeners'. For those who want to stay nearer Palma, the 60-room Punta Negra (owned by Trusthouse Forte) is in a fabulous position on the Costa de Bendinat, away from the hordes but still reasonably convenient. Further away along the south coast, a simple but popular hotel is the Cala Santanyi in the village of the same name. The building is a white arc so that all rooms have a view of one of the most perfect bays imaginable (Tel (971) 680762). Further round the coast is the white holiday complex of Cala d'Or.

Menorca, the smaller neighbour of Mallorca, is a different kettle of fish. Unlike Mallorca, it has escaped mass hotel-building and is still a quiet family holiday island with numerous unspoilt beaches. Of the few hotels, the 75-room Port Mahón is a comfortable, old-fashioned place overlooking the Mahón harbour, praised for its excellent friendly service (Tel (971) 362600); the Rocamar at nearby Cala Fonduco is a restaurant with rooms, providing some of the best seafood on the island and good-value accommodation (Tel (971) 365601).

Ibiza, smaller though more touristy than Menorca, has a Moorish feel to it – the last vestiges of its 8thC occupation. One of the island's few luxury hotels is the Hacienda. The setting is lovely and the facilities are extensive (see page 178). El Palacio (see page 178) is especially for film buffs. Pike's (Tel (971) 342222) is a secluded country house popular with pop stars.

Formentera is a tiny island off the south coast of Ibiza. History and tourism have left it virtually untouched, and it has endless deserted beaches served by a handful of hotels. The choice is mainly between small and simple, such as the 20-room Sa Volta at Es Pujols (Tel (971) 328125), and big and smart, such as the 330-room La Mola at Es Arenals (Tel (971) 328069).

Taking pets abroad
Although our fact boxes state whether pets are accepted by hotels, residents of Britain should be aware that they should not be tempted to take theirs abroad. The difficulty arises when returning to Britain: because of the risk of bringing an animal infected with rabies, most animals would have to go into a long period of quarantine.

Mallorca

Town house hotel, Binissalem

Scott's

Calm, sophistication and unobtrusive luxury are the hallmarks of the new breed of upmarket 'house' hotels which we find in many fashionable cities: now the unspoilt Mallorcan hinterland can boast one as well. Binissalem is the wine capital of the island, a quiet Medieval town ideally situated just 20 minutes from Palma, 30 minutes from excellent beaches and golf clubs on both coasts and close to the island's beautiful mountains. It is a newcomer to this latest edition of the guide.

In keeping with the genre, a discreet brass plaque is the only sign that the elegant former merchant's house in the town's small main square is a hotel. Inside, nothing disappoints; the interior is as calm, sophisticated and unobtrusively luxurious as you could wish, especial attention having been paid to the twelve bedrooms. Each one is different, although they all display the same high standards, with charming fabrics, furniture and pictures, as well as fresh flowers. The beds are top-quality handmade and feel it, with pure cotton sheets and delicious goose-down pillows (synthetic ones are on offer to those who suffer from allergies). Breakfasts are suitably sumptuous, served either in your room, in the breakfast room or on the terrace. A pampering treat.

Nearby mountains; Palma 12 miles (19 km).

Plaza de la Iglesia 12, 07350 Binissalem, Mallorca
Tel (971) 870100
Fax (971) 870267
Location in central square; ample parking
Meals breakfast; light evening meals
Prices rooms PPPP
Rooms 10 double and suites, 2 single, all with bath; all rooms have central heating, phone, satellite TV/video on request, hairdrier
Facilities 4 sitting rooms, breakfast room, bar/bistro, spa pool, terraces
Credit cards MC, V
Children welcome over 12
Disabled access difficult
Pets not accepted
Closed never
Proprietors George Scott and Judy Brabner Scott

Mallorca

Hotel La Residencia

Almost everything about the Residencia (owned by Richard Branson) is out of the ordinary. Set above the road at the north end of the fashionable village of Deia, it is a cluster of creeper-covered stone buildings in beautiful tiered gardens. The core of the hotel is a 16thC manor house; its original olive mill is now the restaurant. There is also an annexe above the swimming-pool behind the main hotel, built in the same pink stone with white shutters.

The interior of the hotel is exquisitely furnished with antique pieces, colourful rugs and fascinating modern art. Bedrooms vary in size – from smallish singles to an enormous suite in a sep-arate building. All have lovely wooden furniture and many have antique or four-poster beds. There are bars and breakfast-rooms in both parts of the hotel, though most people eat out on the terraces overlooking either the swimming-pool (surrounded by elegant cypresses and silver birches) or the front lawns.

Another highlight is the hotel's acclaimed restaurant, El Olivo. Its lofty ceiling, dripping candelabra, cane furniture and elegant tables, set among relics of the olive mill, make a wonderfully romantic setting for an excellent four- or eight-course dinner.
Nearby Valldemosa (10 km), Sóller (10 km).

Finca Son Canals 07179, Deia, Mallorca
Tel (971) 639011
Location Signposted from the road from Deia to Soller ; with garden and car parking
Meals breakfast, lunch, dinner
Prices rooms PPPP with break-fast; lunch PP, dinner PPP
Rooms 38 double, 8 single, 15 suites (2 with private pool), all with bath; all rooms have cen-tral heating, air-conditioning, phone, hairdrier, safe
Facilities restaurant, 4 sitting-rooms, 4 bars, dining-room; 2 swimming-pools, 2 tennis courts, private cove; beauty salon, gymnasium
Credit cards AE, MC, V
Children welcome
Disabled no special facilities
Pets small dogs accepted
Closed never;
Managers Marie Aastrup

Mallorca

Seaside hotel, Port d'Andratx

Villa Italia

From the far side of the bay, the hotel looks very much like a Florentine villa. It was built in the heady 1920s at the whim of an eccentric Italian multimillionaire who wanted to give his lover something more than a string of pearls.

Today Villa Italia is arguably the closest thing to Beverly Hills-on-sea. Politicians, actresses and pop stars have enjoyed a glass of champagne in its swimming-pool and a stroll among the oleanders and palm trees in the gardens.

With its stucco ceilings, Portuguese marble floors, Cretonne curtains, Roman capitals and plinths, mirrors, alabaster chalices, round baths, linen sheets, lace pillows and other hand-made details it is indulgence all the way. For something extra special, if money is no object, book the royal suite.

Service is personal – everything you would expect. An elevator and a small funicular railway transport the luggage to the rooms above.

The area around Andratx (a small, low-key town) is one of the less-developed parts of the Mallorcan coast with some fine cliff-top walks, where Northern Europeans, in particular, will enjoy the specialized and varied wild flowers.

Nearby Dragonera Isle (by boat); Palma de Mallorca (22 km).

Camino de San Carlos, 13, 07157, Port d'Andratx, Mallorca
Tel (971) 674011
Fax (971) 673350
Location on a slope on the south of the bay, badly sign-posted; garden and car parking
Meals breakfast, lunch, dinner
Prices rooms PPPP, including breakfast; meals PP
Rooms 10 double, 6 suites, all with bath; all rooms have air-conditioning, telephone, minibar, TV (satellite)
Facilities restaurant; terraces, swimming-pool, sauna
Credit cards AE, MC, V
Children welcome
Disabled access difficult
Pets not accepted
Closed never
Manager Antonio Martín

Mallorca

Town hotel, Cala Ratjada

Hotel Ses Rotges

Some years ago it might have been a surprise to find a well-established French-run hotel in the middle of this village on Mallorca's east coast. Today it would come as no surprise at all – Cala Ratjada is now a lively cosmopolitan holiday town. The Tétards have kept pace with the local development, cleverly extending their pink-stone hotel in the same style as the original buildings, with arched windows and wrought iron balconies.

The hotel, on the corner of two quiet streets near the beach, overlooks a quiet internal courtyard – a wonderful place to relax among trailing plants, overhanging bougainvillaea and a profusion of colourful flowers. The popular restaurant adjoins the courtyard and is set with red and white tables under a beamed roof. In winter, dinner is served inside in another large, cheerful room. The oldest part of the building, around the original chimney, is now a cosy sitting-room. The bedrooms are spacious and airy; they are supposed to be 'individually furnished', but the ones we saw all had the same tiled floors, wooden furniture and bedheads, star-shaped mirrors and modern bathrooms.

Food is a highlight, earning one of the island's very few Michelin stars.

Nearby Artà (10 km); Manacor (30 km).

Rafael Blanes 21, 07590, Cala Ratjada, Mallorca
Tel (971) 563108
Location in quiet street 200m from beach; with car parking in street
Meals breakfast, lunch, dinner
Prices rooms PP-PPP; breakfast P; meals PP
Rooms 18 double, 2 single, one family room, 3 suites, all with bath; all rooms have central heating, air-conditioning, phone, TV, safe
Facilities bar, dining-room, sitting-room, TV room, patio
Credit cards AE, DC, MC, V
Children tolerated
Disabled access generally difficult; one ground-floor room
Pets not accepted
Closed end Nov to 1 Mar
Proprietor Gérard Charles Tétard

Mallorca

Country hotel, Valldemosa

Vistamar de Valldemosa

Vistamar is an appropriate name for this lovely old villa set in countryside on rocky cliffs – you get tantalizing glimpses of the sea through the tangle of pines and olives in front of the hotel. Paths go some way down the cliffs; you cannot get right down to the cove from here, but then you don't really need to – the hotel has its own spectacularly positioned swimming-pool, and is only minutes away from the delightful port of Valldemosa.

A stone archway leads under a balustraded balcony (impressively lit at night) into a cobbled courtyard, with the rooms of the hotel set around three sides. The atmosphere inside is of absolute calm. Rooms are beamed and have heavy wooden doors and antique furniture. Comfortable green and white sofas and chairs are dotted around the two white-walled sitting-rooms, and interesting modern art adds a splash of colour. Dinner is served either inside, or in the partly glassed-in terrace overlooking the gardens.

Bedrooms, some of which have large sun terraces, are cool and comfortable, with spotless white bathrooms, linen bedcovers and massive wooden cupboards. There are further examples of modern art along the walls of the tall corridors.

Nearby Valldemosa; Bañalbufar (15 km); Deia (15 km).

Carretera Andraitx km2
07170, Valldemosa, Mallorca
Tel (971) 612300
Fax (971) 612583
Location on flat olive plain, 2.5km W of Valldemosa; with garden and car parking
Meals breakfast, lunch, dinner
Prices rooms PPPP with breakfast; breakfast P; meals PPP
Rooms 16 double, all with bath; all rooms have central heating, phone, TV, minibar; a few rooms have jacuzzi
Facilities dining-rooms, sitting-rooms, bar, terrace; swimming-pool
Credit cards AE, DC, MC, V
Children accepted
Disabled access difficult
Pets not accepted
Closed Nov to Jan
Proprietor Pedro Coll

Mallorca

Country hotel, Orient

Hotel L'Hermitage

The great attraction of L'Hermitage is its setting – tucked away in a beautiful fruit-growing valley in the mountains, miles from the beaten track (no mean achievement in Mallorca). It consists of a somewhat strange selection of buildings: a narrow 17thC stone manor house (with tower), a two-storey modern block overlooking an orchard and a totally separate cloister with 16 twisted stone pillars enclosing lemon and orange trees. Only four of the bedrooms are in the old house. These have tiny windows peering out of thick walls, making the rooms beautifully cool but also very dim; with polished furniture on old tiled floors, they have much more character than the modern rooms – though these are also cool and comfortable, with palatial bathrooms.

There is a warren of tiny public rooms in the old part of the hotel, including an elegant downstairs sitting-room and a cosy upstairs one with an open fire. In contrast, the dining-room in the old olive mill is enormous. It still has a sloping, beamed ceiling and the original grinding-stones, which make an admirable table for the generous buffet breakfasts. Outside, there is a terrace lined with tables, a swimming-pool among the pine trees and two tennis courts are found on the far side of the orchards.
Nearby Buñola (10 km), Alaró (10 km).

07349, Orient, Mallorca
Tel (971) 180303
Fax (971) 180411
Location in fruit-orchard valley in mountains, 1km E of Orient; with garden and car parking
Meals breakfast, lunch, dinner
Prices rooms PPPP; breakfast P; meals *à la carte*
Rooms 24 double, all with bath; all rooms have phone, minibar; some rooms have central heating, TV, safe, hairdrier
Facilities dining-room, 2 sitting-rooms, bar, terrace; sauna, tennis court, swiming-pool
Credit cards AE, DC, MC, V
Children accepted
Disabled no special facilities
Pets not accepted
Closed Nov to Feb
Managers Otto & Franciska Sigrist

Ibiza

Hotel Hacienda Na Xamena

Reached by one of the prettiest lanes on Ibiza, Hotel Hacienda also enjoys one of the most fortunate locations on the island, and is surrounded by crags and pine woods. The terrace around the large, curvacious swimming-pool (one of three) hangs over a spectacular, rocky cove which is accessible only by a scramble. The hotel is built in bright, white Ibizenco style with many arches and rounded corners, and is arranged around a leafy central patio. All rooms have magnificent views. The poolside restaurant has an enviable local reputation. A luxurious and secluded place in which to take refuge from the tourist traps of Ibiza.

Nearby Can Marça cave; Ibiza (23 km).

Na Xamena, San Miguel, Ibiza 07800
Tel (971) 334605
Fax (971) 334606
Location a left turning before the port of San Miguel; car parking
Meals breakfast, lunch, dinner
Prices rooms PPPP; breakfast PP; meals PPP
Rooms 37 double, 5 single, 10 suites; all rooms have central heating, air-conditioning, telephone, minibar, radio, TV (satellite) **Facilities** 2 restaurants, bar; discotheque; swimming-pools (one heated), tennis-court, mountain bikes
Credit cards AE, DC, MC, V
Children welcome
Disabled access possible
Pets accepted in room only
Closed Nov to Easter Week
Manager Sabine Lipszyc

El Palacio

'The Hotel of the Movie Stars', El Palacio is a mecca for film buffs. Every room is named after a legendary Hollywood star. Marilyn Monroe has the two top rooms (and penthouse terrace) which can be booked together as a suite. This ancient, converted mansion in the city's old quarter (peaceful, but five minutes' walk from the nightlife), is decorated throughout with posters, photographs and movie memorabilia, including the only award James Dean received in his lifetime. The hotel's brochure describes not only every room, but also gives the biographies of the eponymous stars and the history of the objects on display.

Nearby Dalt Vila (old town), Cova Santa (8 km).

Calle de la Conquista, 2, Ibiza, Baleares
Tel (971) 301478
Fax (971) 391581
Location in a quiet street in the old town; car parking on street
Meals breakfast, snacks
Prices rooms PPPP including breakfast
Rooms 7 suites, all with bath; all rooms have balcony or terrace. Marilyn suite has hall/kitchen
Facilities sitting-rooms/foyer with video, bar; garden
Credit cards AE, DC, V
Children accepted
Disabled access difficult
Pets small ones only
Closed Nov to Mar
Proprietor Marlise Etienne

Index of hotel names

Hotels are arranged in order of the most distinctive part of their name; other parts of the name are also given, except that very common prefixes such as 'Hotel' and 'La' are omitted. The abbreviation PT is used for Parador de Turismo de España (see Introduction for further explanation). Hotels covered in the several Area introductions, and in the feature boxes on Paradores, are not indexed.

Index of hotel names

Index of hotel names

Index of hotel names

Index of hotel names

Index of hotel locations

In this index, hotels are arranged by the name of the city, town or village they are in or near. Where a hotel is located in a very small place, it may be indexed under a nearby place which is more easily found on maps. The abbreviation PT is used for Parador de Turismo de España (see Introduction for further explanation).

Index of hotel locations

C

D

E

F

G

Index of hotel locations

Index of hotel locations

O

P

R

S

Index of hotel locations

Index of hotel locations

Y

Z

Special offers

Buy your **Charming Small Hotel Guide** by post directly from the publisher and you'll get a worthwhile discount. *

Titles available:	Retail price	Discount price
Austria	£9.99	**£8.50**
Britain & Ireland	£9.99	**£8.50**
Britain: Bed & Breakfast	£9.99	**£8.50**
USA: Florida	£9.99	**£8.50**
France	£9.99	**£8.50**
France: *Bed & Breakfast*	£8.99	**£7.50**
Germany	£8.99	**£7.50**
Italy	£8.99	**£8.50**
USA: New England	£8.99	**£7.50**
Paris	£9.99	**£8.50**
Southern France	£9.99	**£7.50**
Spain	£8.99	**£8.50**
Switzerland	£7.99	**£6.50**
Tuscany & Umbria	£9.99	**£8.50**
Venice & North-east Italy	£9.99	**£8.50**

Also available: Duncan Petersen's **Versatile/ Travel Planner & Guides:** outstanding all-purpose travel guides.

Titles available:	Retail price	Discount price
Australia	£12.99	**£8.75**
California *Travel Planner & Guide*	£12.99	**£8.75**
Central Italy *The Versatile Guide*	£12.99	**£8.75**
Florida *Travel Planner & Guide*	£12.99	£8.75
France *The Versatile Guide*	£12.99	**£8.75**
Greece *The Versatile Guide*	£12.99	**£8.75**
Italy *The Versatile Guide*	£12.99	**£8.75**
Spain *The Versatile Guide*	£12.99	**£8.75**
Thailand *The Versatile Guide*	£12.99	**£8.75**
Turkey *The Versatile Guide*	£12.99	**£8.75**

Please send your order to:

Book Sales, Duncan Petersen Publishing Ltd,
31 Ceylon Road, London W14 OPY
enclosing: 1) the title you require and number of copies
2) your name and address 3) your cheque made out to:
Duncan Petersen Publishing Ltd
*Offer applies to UK only.